D0241823

Getting Through!

HOW TO MAKE WORDS
WORK FOR YOU

GODFREY HOWARD

David & Charles
Newton Abbot   London   North Pomfret (Vt)

British Library Cataloguing in Publication Data
Howard, Godfrey
  Getting through.
  1. Oral communication
  I. Title
  808'.042   PN412/

ISBN 0-7153-7821-X

© Godfrey Howard 1980

All rights reserved. No part of this
publication may be reproduced, stored
in retrieval system, or transmitted,
in any form or by any means, electronic,
mechanical, photocopying, recording or
otherwise, without the prior permission
of David & Charles (Publishers) Limited

Typesetting by ABM Typographics Ltd, Hull
and printed in Great Britain
by Redwood Burn Ltd, Trowbridge & Esher
for David & Charles (Publishers) Limited
Brunel House, Newton Abbot, Devon

Contents

For Françoise Legrand

Introduction

What will this book do for you?

It could change your whole attitude toward using words. The old way starts off with: 'What do I want to say?' This book is about the new way, which always begins with the question: 'What results do I want?' The difference it makes can be astonishing.

Nearly every time you pick up your ballpen, sit down at your typewriter, put your feet up and dictate to your secretary, go in to talk to the boss, rise to your feet in the House of Commons or address the nation from your desk in the White House, you are using words to do something.

Words can get you the job you want, get your complaint dealt with quickly and fairly, get you out of trouble, sell your car or your house, raise capital, increase sales, make something happen or not happen, persuade someone to marry you or just have dinner with you.

We know thousands of words in English plus the syntax of the language, which is how to combine those words into sentences. We can now move on to the next stage: how to make the best possible use of that knowledge in work and relationships—how to use words to get through.

At school we learn vocabulary, spelling and grammar, and are left to get on with the rest of it. It is like learning the Highway Code and the principle of the internal combustion engine, without ever learning to drive a car on a motorway or in heavy traffic. This book puts you behind the driving-wheel of the language, so that it takes you where you want to go.

Words in a dictionary are like objects in a museum: they are interesting but they don't do anything. When words are used in communication, they come to life and go to work for us.

In this book you see what happens when words are in action

in all the different ways of communicating, from letters to advertising, to television, radio, sermons, to speaking to your wife, your husband, the person you work for or the people who work for you. You will link ideas and principles together to build up an understanding of how to use words successfully so they deliver the results you want.

Whatever form it takes, communication that gets good results uses, consciously or unconsciously, the same principles. By seeing how these work in different media and different situations, we can understand them and use them ourselves.

This is not a book about writing good English in a grammatical or academic sense. Other people, from Samuel Johnson and Noah Webster to the Fowler brothers and Eric Partridge, have already done that for their times, although books like theirs will continually need to be written. English is well and living in a lot of different countries, so it is constantly changing; every few years we need a check-up on the language.

At times anyone can feel uncertain about grammar or how to use certain words. Too often these feelings derive from an old-fashioned belief in rigid fixed principles: there are still hardliners who believe that teaching English is teaching dos and don'ts. Such fetters cannot be clamped on to a language as free and volatile as ours. Chapter 11, 'Good and bad English', blows away a lot of old cobwebs and offers guidelines on how to adapt to changes in the use of English now and in the future.

But in no way is this a textbook. It was written using the insight and ideas of many people who are confronted every day in their work and lives by the pressure to use words to get results (see the list at the end of the book). Its aim is to help everyone to make his or her way against the odds, because the odds are usually put up by other people whom we have to convince and persuade before we can move on.

Most of us need this help one way or another, whether we are university graduates or started careers straight from school. A large vocabulary is no guarantee that anyone can use words successfully: it can even be a barrier to getting through.

If you want words to do a great job for you, the first step is to understand how communication works and how human beings are affected by it. So I have brought together the experience of people who are outstandingly successful at using words to deliver the goods. Among them are some of the top advertising people in the world, chairmen and presidents of companies, successful writers, well-known broadcasters, Members of Parliament, senators, even bishops and millionaire song-writers. Some of them have an almost magic touch when it comes to putting across a message and you will find here the best advice they can give.

For the first time, the secrets and techniques of advertising are applied to our ordinary day-to-day problems of using words in any situation. Because according to Marshall McLuhan, who has revolutionary ideas about media and communication, 'historians will find that the ads of our time reflect the range of activities'.

Top copywriters in big London advertising agencies can get paid £30,000 a year plus a lot of other benefits. In New York they can earn as much as film stars. Over a year copywriters do not write all that much but they know how to use words to attract, to convince and to sell. We find out what we can learn from them.

And it's not guesswork. Research companies are employed to test copy, to see whether the ideas come across, TV commercials are screened in front of sample audiences, and probed for factual and psychological impact. Add to that the most important test of all: is the product selling, are proposals being accepted, are the words getting results?

In these ways we learn what works and what does not work. We learn that the difference between knowing how to use words and just having a go can make a difference of hundreds of thousands of pounds to companies, can affect the fortunes of individuals, the success of causes and even the way of the world.

We do not have to believe that the values and attitudes of our society always relate to the pursuit of happiness. That is something else. But if we live in the world, then we need to know how to survive in it; and learning to communicate effectively is right in the front line.

This book is a survival kit. To be successful, or even just to get by, generally requires us to be able to influence other people at times. We might use words for our own good, or to help someone, or for a cause we believe in, or for the good of our country, or the good of mankind. Whatever the reason, everything here is aimed at helping you to get through to people.

The help in this book is meant to be warm and friendly and the ideas easy to take in. It needs a lot of effort to overcome the anxieties and difficulties of life—why add to that?

It all works. Most of the ideas are simple. They are all taken from the direct experience of people who are outstanding at using words to get results. And everything has been tested in the toughest of all laboratories: the market place of goods, ideas, proposals and causes.

1 The Superlanguage

Sixty per cent of the world's radio programmes and seventy per cent of all the letters written in the world every day are in English. So the fact that you can read this book gives you a headstart. You know the most valuable language on earth. If you were born in Great Britain, the United States, Australia, Canada, New Zealand, South Africa or in any other country where the English language is your birthright, you are sitting on a fabulous asset.

The language you speak without effort is the number one language of the twentieth century. In Paris, Rome, Naples, Tokyo, Hamburg, Stockholm, Tel Aviv and in every other large city, teaching English is big business. A recent survey in Denmark showed English as the language that nearly one hundred per cent of all parents wanted their children to learn. Everywhere men and women are working flat out and paying high fees to get a share of the linguistic riches that were dropped straight into your lap.

When you know English, the way is open to the most marvellous literature in the world. The miracle of Shakespeare alone takes care of that. He even helped to make the language for us.

If you 'have seen better days' and are 'poor but honest'; or 'haven't slept a wink' because someone has 'made you mad'; if something is 'all Greek to you' or simply 'neither here nor there'; when 'there is method in your madness' and 'last but not least', 'to tell the truth and shame the devil', 'your heart's desire' is to 'have a charmed life' and to be 'as sound as a bell', because it is 'cold comfort' to be told 'you can only die once'— you are not just speaking English, you are speaking Shakespeare.

If the God of Literature has only one divine son, it is Shakespeare. And he wrote in English.

English offers you a bigger choice of words than most other languages. In French-English, English-French dictionaries, the English-French section is thicker. The *Concise Cambridge Italian Dictionary* has three hundred pages for Italian-English but five hundred for English-Italian.

English is rich in words because history has made it a melting-pot of a language. It started life as a modest dialect brought to England in the fifth century by Germanic tribes. Judging by the many early English place-names in the south of England and the Midlands, these tribes spread across the country, taking their language with them.

In 1066, the best remembered date in English history, came the Norman Conquest, which led to English getting thoroughly mixed up with Norman French. Our vocabulary took on vast shiploads of words from the mainstream of Romance languages, so that we can now recognise thousands of words in French, Italian, Spanish and other languages descended from Latin.

Caxton and his English printing press about 1475 took English a big step forward; books could be produced faster and cheaper than manuscripts. A hundred years later and on into the seventeenth century, English basked and stretched in the warmth and glory of Elizabethan England, making and being made by Shakespeare and the Authorised Version of the Bible.

The eighteenth century, with its scientific outlook, disciplined and polished English, as it became the language of reason and philosophy. Then around the mid-1800s, in smug Victorian England, English looked as if it might settle down complacently, which is the worst thing that can happen to any language or to any human being.

But before this hardening of the arteries set in, along came a transfusion of rich vigorous new blood from America, a linguistic lease-lend of young colourful words that has been shaking up the language ever since. More than any other language, English has been kept on its toes and has become the most lively and versatile language in the world.

Let's not fool ourselves that all the people who want to learn our language care about these things. For most of them, this is what really counts: English comes first by a long way at doing the very thing for which language came into being—to communicate with other people. No other language is understood by such a diversity of people in so many different countries.

Anybody who wants to be somebody on the international scene must know English. In the United Nations' buildings in New York and Geneva and in UNESCO in Paris, English is the language you hear most.

Any important book written in another language is soon translated into English. English is the international language of aviation and the obligatory language, or at least a smattering of it, of every waiter, taxi-driver and air hostess.

Hungary, Italy, Japan, Mexico, Peru, and on into half the other countries of the world, are adding to their vocabularies hundreds of English words, so more and more of our words are international. In Panama, a puncture is called a *flataya*. In Paris, they 'cherchent le *parking* pour faire le *shopping* pour le *weekend*'.

Pre-war English-French dictionairies translated 'week-end' as *le bout de la semaine*. Now you say *le weekend* as well as *le gadget, le cornflakes, le pullover, le marketing, le know-how, le check-up* and *le jogging*.

Even the Berlin Wall cannot hold back the advance. At an East German bar you can get an orange juice by asking for an *Apfelsinemsaft*, if you know the word, but you might as well take it easy and say *Ein Juice*.

Record shops all over the world sell *singles* or *LPs*. There is only one language of pop music and that's English.

English is so successful because it is also the language of the United States. But ask Americans what language they speak and the answer will be *English*. English, the language of Stoke-on-Trent and Stoke Newington, of Old Sodbury and the Old Kent Road, the language of Chelsea Pensioners, Oxford dons,

Wiltshire farmers, the Archbishop of Canterbury and John Lennon.

If it is also the language that Bing Crosby crooned in, President Carter declares in, the language you hear on the New York subway, on the Mississippi River and in so many other expected and unexpected places, from the Australian outback to the road to Katmandu, we can all be grateful for the number and variety of places and people where and by whom we are understood.

English is the superlanguage, because it gets through to more people in more countries than any other language in the world.

All we have to do is to use it.

2 Making words work harder for you

How do you go about writing a letter that a lot depends on?

Do you first decide what you want to say and then write it out in rough? Or perhaps you dictate a draft off the top of your head. You go over it, changing a word here and there, taking this out, putting that in and turning a sentence round so that it sounds better. The chances are you are working within the same habitual pattern of using words. There is no real breakthrough.

Yet the words we use play a big part in our contacts with people and turn things one way or the other for us. These may not be real values; but in the rough and tumble of life we cannot help reacting to words that are written and said to us, just as others react to our words.

Even in intimate human relationships, we need to find the right words at the right time. Take a man coming home late for dinner or a woman keeping a man waiting. Communication can work—or not work.

The last time John came home late, there was a row. His wife was hungry, the meal spoilt and he hadn't phoned her. Again he lets himself in through the front door and calls out 'I'm sorry I'm late, darling'. That's exactly what he said last time. You could hardly expect it to succeed now and produce a relaxed drink, after a hard day in the office or whatever, and a quiet peaceful dinner later on.

The difference between the way most people use words and the way an athlete works at improving his track record is that the athlete is never satisfied. He knows that by analysing his technique and making changes he can improve his performance. That is the only way to think about words, if you want to be good at using them.

The president of an advertising agency in Los Angeles pitches for new business by asking advertisers if they are satisfied with the results they are getting from their present advertising. If the answer is *no*, the door is wide open for him to talk about moving their account to his agency.

But if the answer is *yes*, he follows up with this question:

Have you ever considered that you might be able to get fifty per cent more results from the same expenditure? It's worth looking at, isn't it?

His agency regularly adds new clients to its list of accounts.

Generally they do step up results, sometimes by much more than fifty per cent. One reason is that they take a new look at what had become an old problem. By starting afresh, free from hang-ups over old ideas, they focus as sharply as possible on the *results* they want. Just from that, it often follows that the new advertising is much more successful.

This is a clue to the first step, and it is a very big step, towards making words work harder for you. Shift your focus from 'What do I want to say?' to *'What results do I want?'*

When it's results we're after, we should forget about expressing ourselves and concentrate on getting through to the other person. The two things are not the same. Every successful copywriter understands that but not everyone else does. This idea is so simple that it is easy to overlook how much it can do for you. It can change your whole attitude towards using words.

So often a communication is an ego-trip. Remember the man coming home late and calling out *'I'm sorry I'm late, darling'*. Communications like that say: this is how I feel, this is what I want to say, this is what I want you to do for me, this is how frightened I am. The moment you take all that energy and let it loose on what you want your letter, conversation, interview or telephone call to achieve, things start to happen.

Read this application that was sent to the personnel manager of a big company:

I am writing in answer to your advertisement for a secretary/ assistant to your Export Manager.

16

Your advertisement mentions good typing, and although I can type accurately at 60wpm, I want a position where I do not have to type very much.

You also say that a knowledge of French would be an advantage. I do know some French, and would be very glad if the job you are offering would help me to improve it.

I have always wanted to work for a company like yours, because I like all the social contacts you can make in a big organisation. In fact the kind of work I'd really like is a job dealing with people.

I've already booked up my holidays for this year, and the dates are . . .

The letter goes on like that. The personnel manager said wearily 'The only thing left out is what she'd like for lunch!'

The writer of that letter did not get on the short list, although the job might have been just right for her. She could have asked about holidays and all the other things at an interview, which she would have been offered if she'd written:

I can type accurately at 60wpm. But I am also good at dealing with people, so could bring other things to the job, as well as typing. I already know some French and would work hard at learning more in order to help your Export Manager.

It is saying the same thing—but in a very different way.

Even sophisticated and successful people make the same mistake. Alistair Cooke, the famous Anglo-American broadcaster, tells how he was approached by a leading banking corporation about making a television commercial.

On their grand embossed notepaper, he read:

Congratulations! You have been chosen as the image to represent our business.

Does that sound like an ego-trip or doesn't it? According to Mr Cooke, his first impulse was to tell them 'Screw you!' But he turned them down politely, though they were offering a million dollars spread over ten years in return for what would have amounted to one day's work.

Suppose the great banking corporation had directed their letter simply at the result they wanted, to get Alistair Cooke to consider their request. They might have set about it like this:

> We believe that, in the general way, you would not want to make a television commercial.
>
> But some of us here sincerely feel that you personify the kind of integrity that we try to have as a bank. So we are inviting you to consider making a television commercial for us based on a script that we should, of course, agree word for word with you.
>
> The fee we could offer would be generous. It would amount to around $1,000,000 spread over ten years. We should need to take up no more of your time than a day or two.
>
> We all know that money is a temptation although we could well understand that you would not want to be too influenced by it over something like this. It is more important for you to know that our TV commercial will be fair and straightforward.
>
> There may also be causes close to your heart which part of the fee could enable you to support in a way that would not otherwise be possible.
>
> At this stage, would you be prepared to discuss it with us? We'll do our best to satisfy you on any points you want to raise.

I have no idea whether that letter would have made any difference to Mr Cooke. But as the president of the Los Angeles ad agency says, 'It's worth looking at, isn't it?'

This approach introduces into communication the whole concept of *function*. We rate a piece of machinery according to how well it does its job. The simple function of a car is to get us from one place to another safely and economically. When Sir Alec Issigonis' Mini first appeared in 1959, it obviously put function first. The transverse engine took up so little room, that nearly all the space was available for carrying passengers. The result was an overnight and long-lasting success.

A car designed to satisfy our egos would not function as well. It may be less economic and even less safe. We are often prepared to accept that, if we want a car to impress our friends, compensate for a feeling of inadequacy or make us feel young. We get what we want and we pay the price for it.

It is the same with words. We may want to let off steam or assert ourselves. But if instead our communication has to influence someone, to get people to do something for us or for others, or to accept a point of view, then our words will work much harder if we turn them away from ourselves and point them towards the result we want.

As soon as you analyse the function of a communication, whatever form it takes, you start looking at words in a new way. A communication becomes a piece of machinery and the first question is: Will it work? H. G. Wells, who achieved what he wanted in life through words, said that 'language is an implement quite as much as an implement of stone and steel'. I borrow that analogy gratefully and offer it as a valuable way to look at any act of purposeful communication.

This is what happens when a letter is aimed simply and accurately at getting results. Like most of the examples in this book, what follows actually happened.

A man invited his girl friend to spend the night in his flat. The next morning, while she was taking a shower, she dropped a heavy glass bottle of toilet water and it cracked the shower tray.

The man was calm and collected and said it didn't matter at all. But that's not how he felt. The tray was fixed into a recess with quarry tiles cemented in all round. To put in a new tray meant that everything had to be hacked out and replaced. The heavy bottle of toilet water had been a gift from him to her, which didn't make him feel any better.

The first thing he did was to send in a claim to his insurance company and keep his fingers crossed. After the usual delay he received the following reply:

> Thank you for your letter dated the 17th August together with the completed claim form.
> We have to advise you that this accidental damage does not constitute a claim under the terms and conditions of the Policy, as accidental damage of shower trays is not covered.

When he read the policy carefully, he saw that it listed baths, wash basins, sinks and WC pans, but not a word about shower trays. A phone call to his insurance brokers confirmed that he did not have a case.

He wanted to write to the insurance company calling them a load of sharks, low-lives and con-men. That would have made him feel better, until he got the bill for the repair. The estimate came to £250 or so, a lot to him but nothing much to insurance companies. So he directed every word in his letter towards the result he wanted:

> I have received your letter rejecting my claim because you do not consider that the terms of the Policy include accidental damage to shower trays.
> I sincerely believe that this is not fair. It looks as if the wording in the Policy goes back a number of years to a time when showers were uncommon. So it doesn't mention them.
> You will agree that nowadays more and more people have showers, and that they are not at all exceptional. They are even officially recommended as a way of saving fuel.
> Because it seems to me that I am being penalised by an unintentional omission from your Policy, I feel justified in making a complaint of unfair treatment to the British Insurance Association.
> You are such an old and well-known insurance company, that before doing this it seems reasonable to write to you first to see if you will reconsider my claim.

It is all straightforward and quiet. Let us take it apart and see why it works so well.

He starts off by quoting their reasons for rejecting his claim. Then he lets them off the hook by suggesting that the wording of the policy may be out of date by chance rather than intention. Next he makes a statement that they have to agree with, which is that showers are common these days. The threat about complaining to the British Insurance Association is to make sure his letter is taken seriously.

At the end he treats them with respect by asking to have his claim reconsidered. That puts them in a superior position— they have to 'consider' something. The reply came quickly:

> We are in receipt of your communication dated 7th September.
> We apologise for excluding the shower as of course under present day fittings showers would be covered.
> A cheque for the sum of £250 will follow.

And it did.

The man is a well known copywriter, so he knew what he was about. It had taken him an hour to write his letter, which makes it his best hourly rate ever—even in advertising.

His letter is a well designed instrument of communication, constructed to function efficiently, which it did. It is a valuable model for any situation when you have to try to get something put right or reconsidered. At first glance it seems a simple letter; but the Mini looked like a simple car.

It is not often that a poet writes for results. Andrew Marvell (1621-78) wrote poetry but he was also a politician writing newsletters to his constituents and pamphlets attacking the government. He could use words for action.

Marvell was faced with the problem of what was called, in the seventeenth century, a coy mistress. We would say a reluctant virgin. He wrote a love poem to her, but not one full of how *he* felt and what *he* longed for. Instead he designed it step by step, as a means to an end: to persuade his girl to come across. There's no need to give it in full here, because if you are not already familiar with it, you can find it in many anthologies.

Marvell says that if there were all the time in the world, his girl could wait as long as she wants before going to bed with him. But it's not like that; time is never on our side:

> . . . at my back I always hear
> Time's wingéd chariot hurrying near:
> And yonder all before us lie
> Deserts of vast eternity.
> Thy beauty shall no more be found;
> Nor, in thy marble vault, shall sound
> My echoing song: then worms shall try
> That long preserv'd virginity:
> And your quaint honour turn to dust;
> And into ashes all my lust.

It is quiet and elegant, with nice seventeenth-century turns of phrase. But the cutting-edge is as sharp as a razor:

> The grave's a fine and private place,
> But none I think do there embrace.
> *Now*, therefore, while the youthful hue
> Sits on thy skin like morning dew,
> And while thy willing soul transpires
> At every pore with instant fires,
> *Now* let us sport us while we may!

The principles of communication for results have always been the same. Marvell defined what he wanted and never lost sight of it. His poem is a fine example of writing for results. I should like to add that it was successful; but literary scholars have never bothered to find out. It deserved to work; and well chosen lines from it have been used many times since to help out other men—and also women.

There is no need to think that writing for results cannot be done with style and humour. We can read Marvell's poem for its wit and imaginative use of English, as well as for a lesson in making words work.

When you are writing, you can think as long as you like. But to say the right thing at the right moment, you have to think quickly. If you focus on the result you want, there is a much better chance that the right words will come into your head.

Arthur Pinero's play, *The Second Mrs Tanqueray*, which opened at London's St James's Theatre in 1893, was revolutionary, different from anything the public had seen before. Pinero was on edge, and while the first act was on, he went for a walk in St James's Park. He came back in time for the interval and Mrs Patrick Campbell, the actress playing the lead, asked the question actresses have always asked: 'How was I?'

Pinero could have said that he was too worried to watch. That would have been thinking of himself. But he wanted the actress to go back on stage for Act Two with confidence. He replied:

> If you can play the second act, my dear, as marvellously as you played Act One, then we shall have the greatest success of all time.

22

The Second Mrs Tanqueray made a reputation and a lot of money for both of them. Bernard Shaw, who was in the audience, said it was the most sensational début of the century.

It's not easy to find just the right words at the moment we need them. It's much easier to think of them as we are going down the stairs on the way out. The telephone can often put us on the spot. We are caught on the hop and cannot think quickly enough. But if you apply the same principle, it will work. Think of the result you want and do not lose sight of it.

In a small company, production looked like being held up by essential parts not coming through. The production manager telephoned the suppliers. They wanted to look into it before they could give him a definite answer. But he knew what he wanted:

Can you find out within an hour? . . .
Say two hours then? . . .
Good. It's now 3 o'clock. I won't budge from my office until 5.
Can you call back during that time? . . .
Thank you very much.

Unexpectedly a friend calls you long distance. She is very upset. It is hard to know what to say because there is no time to think. But you want to comfort her. Keep that aim in front of you and before you hang up, perhaps you will say something like, 'I'll think of you every day.'

The trick in every communication, that has to work for you or help someone else, is to project the words away from yourself and on to the result you want. This principle comes up time and again because it is a psychological truth that a new insight must be repeated many times before it becomes part of us.

In big advertising agencies all over the world there are men and women who can evaluate words in relation to overall marketing plans and objectives. If they are good at their job, they focus clearly on the result the advertising has to achieve.

When advertising fails, it is often because results have taken second place to something else. At creative meetings in ad agencies, writers and art directors are sometimes carried away

23

by their own ideas. They are off on an ego-trip; and if they take everyone else along with them, the advertising may look brilliant or beautiful, but it can be wasteful or a complete disaster.

The best advertising comes when creative originality is harnessed to a clear purpose. Some of the most depressing advertising results from self-indulgence. When we study advertising, it helps us to be more objective in our own use of words.

Notice when you are stopped by an advertisement and start to read it. If it has made you interested in the product advertised, it is working for results. Look at it again to see how it works. If it has simply made you interested for a moment in the advertisement, rather than the product, it is more likely to be an ego-trip than a good piece of communication machinery. Look at that too, to avoid making the same mistake.

To see advertising with no frills but simply directed towards results, turn to the pages in your newspaper given over to mail order advertisements. It is said that the best test of an ad man is writing mail order ads. The cost per reply and the cost per sale are usually worked out exactly. If the same advertisement appears week after week, you know it works. Mail order ads are often rather crude and simplistic, but they reveal the bare bones of communication.

I have seen late-night television shows in Chicago with commercials given 'live' by secondhand-car salesmen. The salesman stood beside the car, talked about it, said how much and knocked it down to the first person to telephone. Communication stripped for action!

When you look at TV commercials, try to see how they are working—or whether they are working at all. Self-indulgence can be very expensive when only fifteen seconds on the box cost thousands of pounds.

Sir Arthur Quiller-Couch, a Cornishman who became Professor of English at Cambridge, wrote a book called *On the Art of Writing*. One of his best bits of advice is 'Murder your darlings!' He means be ruthless with ideas or phrases you fall in love with. They can turn your communication into an ego-trip.

One of the best aimed TV commercials I know was made by Groucho Marx, now making more laughter in heaven. Marx's son, Arthur, had written Groucho's biography. Like a good father, Groucho was promoting the book on television in New York with a series of five-second spots. There seemed to be only one of these short commercials, which was repeated time and time again. But I never got tired of it.

Groucho rolled his eyes, stopped chewing his cigar for a moment and said, 'I hear my son's written my biography. I'd better get outa town—quick!' And he was gone.

This was communication with economy, accuracy and right on target. It made you interested, told you what the book was about and made you want to read it—all in five seconds.

Whenever you are vague or disorganised about the results you want, you are taking a big chance on what happens to your letter, report, telephone call, or at a meeting. Words can do a good job only when they are directed towards a clearly defined end. It is good advice to crystallise the results you want. Crystals are always sharp and defined, with clean-cut facets. That is the perfect way to visualise the results you need from any important communication in any form.

Listen for a moment to how Sir Winston Churchill applied this principle. It is May 1940. Neville Chamberlain has just resigned and Churchill has formed a new administration. He speaks to the House of Commons, for the first time as Prime Minister:

> You ask, What is our aim? I can answer in one word: Victory—victory at all costs, victory in spite of all terror, victory, however long and hard the road may be.

That is crystal clear.

Another politician makes a speech. His aim is to win the election and he knows that his best chance is to go after un-committed voters, because they can be moved one way or the other. This is the beginning of crystallisation; if he works on it further, he will get somewhere.

What happens instead? It is lonely standing up in front of a lot of people. So he talks to his friends, the people who are going to vote for him anyway. He gets a standing ovation, comes away pleased but probably without gaining a single extra vote.

The girl who wrote the letter quoted earlier, applying for the job with the export manager of a big company, was genuinely interested. Her aim very simply was to get an interview and every word of her letter should have been directed towards that.

It is important not to ask a communication to do too much at one go, or we could lose everything. The imaginary letter from the banking corporation to Alistair Cooke was not aimed at getting him to agree to make a television commercial—at least not right away. The first step was to get him to consider it: 'Would you be prepared to discuss it with us?' There is a world of difference between a closed door and an open one.

The man with the broken shower tray did not demand a cheque from the insurance company. He just asked them to reopen the file, which would give him the chance to negotiate with them. It was a bonus when they paid up right away.

When we simplify what we are asking for, it is easier for people to respond. Some of the best advertisements ask only one thing from the reader. On 2 November 1976, readers of *The Times* were stopped by a whole page that was blank, except for a date written in giant letters:

2ND
NOV.
1992

Below was one short sentence and everyone read it:

> Just a small reminder that, according to statistics, anyone buying a new Volvo to-day will probably have to replace it on the above date.

There are other reasons why Volvos are good cars. But whoever wrote that advertisement picked out one good reason. The result was that every reader of *The Times* that day took in that a Volvo lasts a long time. The ad could have said a lot more and people would have come away with a lot less.

Even when we have to say 'no' to someone, it is useful to think through what we want our communication to achieve. Of course we have to make it crystal clear that whoever it is has not got the job, is not going to borrow money from us, get the contract, or stay for the week-end. But if we use our words to help them accept our decision with goodwill, we might make a friend instead of an enemy. Justifying ourselves doesn't help someone else and is often another kind of ego-trip.

Susan Barton applied for a job as secretary to a TV producer. She was asked to go for an interview and did well at a test. A month went by and she heard nothing. Then this letter came:

Secretary to Television Producer
We are writing to inform you that you have not been selected for the above appointment.

That was all. The case for writing a more friendly letter is that we are all human. This time there was another reason, one they didn't know about: Susan's father was a shareholder in the television company. He wrote an angry letter to the chairman.

The letter from the insurance company to the copywriter with the broken shower tray didn't do them any good. It just said *no*. If they had directed their letter in another way, he might have accepted their decision.

This next letter, from a publisher, rejects a novel, but leaves the writer feeling good about it:

I hope you don't think we have kept your novel an unconscionable time but we have been considering it seriously as it deserves. You convey the horrors of living in a corrupt society convincingly and I found the sexual sequences both unembarrassing and strong.

However, the guy has zero lovability which is bad for business. I just don't see how we could sell enough copies in these hardening times to get by, but I really mean that the book being so well written could be publishable elsewhere.

I am sorry to end with an inelegant sentence so unlike your own.

27

In a very different situation, a girl wrote this warm and compassionate letter of rejection:

Dear Bill,
I cannot marry you. Yet I am so moved by your asking me. If this makes you unhappy, as it might do, please forgive me. It is a consolation for me to know that my refusing you now will one day bring so much happiness to another girl, and that will be the girl you do marry.

There are big dividends for yourself and sometimes for others when you refine your ideas about the results you want your words to achieve.

A good tennis player does more than send the ball back across the net. He tries to make it land in the right place. 'The difficulty', said Robert Louis Stevenson, 'is not to affect your reader, but to affect him precisely as you wish.'

It is hard work to write a letter that gets just the right result, so it is useful to keep a file of good letters. You can sometimes adapt a letter, use part of it or let it spark off another idea for any new situation.

We'll go on, in the next chapter, to look at what it is like for the people at the receiving end, who open our letters, answer our telephone calls or sit opposite us at an interview. Before that there is one loose end that was left dangling.

Remember the man coming home late for dinner and faced with a miserable evening? I looked around for someone who had dealt with this situation successfully in real life. There is no one solution to any problem of communication. But we learn from good examples how to find the best way for ourselves. In that spirit, here is the true story of a girl who kept her husband waiting two hours for dinner.

As she let herself in through the front door, she crystallised the results she wanted by deciding that the best thing would be to say something he would agree with. She went straight into him, and said 'You must be starving! And it's all my fault!' He agreed with her. Before long they were having a quiet dinner together.

3 Good communication is like good love-making

There is a simple principle that can double the effectiveness of everything you write. The highest paid advertising writer of all time said it makes one dollar do the work of ten. It functions not only in advertising and in letters, but at meetings, interviews, conversations and even on the telephone. You can apply it every time you write or say things you hope will do something for you or help someone else.

I heard of it in Chicago, in the office of the head of an advertising agency. His name was Fairfax Cone and the business he built up is now world-wide.

That day in Chicago, a writer came in with an ad he had written. Fax, as the boss was called, read it and asked the writer 'Would you say that to someone you know?' It was the most valuable lesson of all in communication.

So much of what we write is to people we have never met. The millions who read advertisements are complete strangers to the people who write them. On the telephone, we often speak to people we don't know. If we write or speak as if those people are strangers, how can they respond to us? Fear of strangers, xenophobia, is a basic fear of mankind and when we are afraid of something we keep away from it.

The first principle of good communication is to treat the other person as a friend. Look them in the eye, in your imagination, and make real contact with them as sharing our human situation. That situation is essentially lonely. Every communication, even about the most ordinary things, is an opportunity to throw a bridge across the void. Then our letters, conversations, speeches and phone calls have more effect than we could have ever believed possible.

Douglas Hurd, who was Edward Heath's political secretary,

says that top politicians must always ask 'How would I explain this if I were sitting in the living-room of one of my constituents?' Peter Hobden, a London copywriter, wants his copy to 'feel warm and comfortable'. Here are three letters that ignore this principle. From a bank manager:

> After your visit here, we considered your request, and regret that, in the light of the securities you are able to provide, we are unable at the present time to agree to the overdraft facilities that you require.

Would you say that to a friend? The woman who received the letter moved her account to another bank. Another, from a driver to the police:

> An officious busy-body of a traffic warden gave me the enclosed parking ticket. She didn't even stop to ask whether I had a good reason for leaving my car parked on double yellow lines. Oh no! She was too busy writing out more parking tickets.

Would you say that to a friend? The driver had to pay the £6 penalty. From a woman to her dentist:

> I have received your account and am enclosing a cheque for half your charges, which is all I intend to pay. The work you did on my two teeth was unsatisfactory. I was in a lot of pain afterwards, and because you were away on holiday, I had to go to another dentist.

Would you say that to a friend? The patient had to pay the fees in full.

Here are those three letters rewritten as one human being talking to another. From the bank manager:

> I enjoyed meeting you and have thought a lot about your request for a loan. Unfortunately, we cannot do it for you, at least not on the basis of the securities you can offer. I'm very sorry, because I know how much it means to you.
>
> Is there any possibility that you can offer better security, such as a personal guarantee from a friend?
>
> You are always welcome to come back here and talk about any ways we can help you. I'll do my best.

There is a good chance the bank would have kept the customer. From the driver:

> Can you please help me? There wasn't time to explain to the traffic warden, who gave me the enclosed parking ticket, why my car had been left on double yellow lines. So may I tell you how it happened and hope you will consider cancelling the penalty?

He might have got off, if there were good reasons for leaving the car there. From the dentist's patient:

> Thank you for your account. I'm so sorry to have to tell you that I had a lot of pain after the fillings, although I know you did your best for me. It was bad luck, because of course I wanted to come back and ask you to look at my teeth. But you were on holiday and all I could do was go to another dentist.
>
> Neither of us could help this, so would you be willing to accept the enclosed cheque for half your fees? As you know now, I have to pay the other dentist as well.
>
> I hope you had a good holiday.

That might have been the end of the matter.

As in those letters, there is often a conflict of interest: you want one thing—the other person wants something else. Your secretary has a date: you want her to stay to type a letter. If it can seem the inevitable outcome of the situation you are both involved in, she can identify herself with the reasons. It could go like this: the letter is to an important customer; if they don't get it tomorrow we could lose the business; will you help to keep it?

A successful order always helps the other person to become identified with the purpose of it. We cannot be all things to all people but if we take time to imagine what it is like to be the other person, they will often meet us half way. Otherwise our communication, whatever form it takes, stands much less chance of getting results—unless we tote a gun.

In *Damn Yankees*, an old musical about baseball, there was a great number to put over the idea that no matter how good a player you are, 'You've gotta have heart!' It's the same with communication. The word 'heart' often comes up in advice about getting through to people. Sir Arthur Quiller-Couch said, 'Good style consists of thinking with the heart as well as the head.' Henri Cartier-Bresson says the art of photography (another form of communication) is 'putting one's head, one's eye and one's heart on the same axis'.

That guru of communication, Alistair Cooke, tells how he finds himself talking to his typewriter, because what he is aiming at is 'the perfect conversational tone of one man talking to another'. For Jane Austen, writing letters was like 'talking almost as fast as I could'.

Sometimes it is a good idea to talk aloud our letters, or anything else we write, and listen to see if we are keeping the reader at arm's length. Or are we friendly and welcoming, like one human being talking to another?

The chief executive of a big international organisation does this when he writes a letter that a lot depends on: he seals it up in an envelope and gets on with something else. After an hour or two, he slits open the envelope and reads the letter. It helps him to feel what it will be like to be at the receiving end.

A senior copywriter in an ad agency on Madison Avenue spends the morning every now and again in a supermarket, looking at the faces of customers and talking to them. He says this is the only way he can get the feeling of what it is like to read ads instead of just writing them. Another copywriter worked as a barman for a week in Milwaukee, before settling down to write advertisements for a new lager. An ad agency avoids what it calls the 'ivory-tower disease' by bringing small groups of agency people and consumers together for group discussions.

President Carter brought together the President of Egypt and the Prime Minister of Israel for a meeting at Camp David, not with an invitation from the Department of State, but with a letter written by hand, as one man to another.

It is easy to forget that every letter we write is read by a person, just as it is always a person who answers whenever we dial a number (answering machines are only a stop-gap). Whether you are writing to ICI, Dupont, the Bank of England or the Coca-Cola Corporation, your letter will be read by one person at a time; and often the say-so of the first person to read it decides what will happen next.

Good communication is like good love-making because both involve us with one other person and the more we are aware of them, the more they will respond. A creative director in Chicago wrote that she thinks of her ads as people—she called her article 'Would Your Daughter Want to Marry This Ad?'

A TV commercial for a tomato paste showed an Italian newly married to a Polish blonde from Cleveland, Ohio. The first time his whole family comes to dinner, of all things she makes an Italian dish—*chicken caccetori*! What can a Polish girl from Cleveland know about Italian cooking?

They are all there waiting: Uncle Guiseppe, Aunt Rosa, Cousin Paulo, Mama, Papa. They give a what-kind-of-food-is-this? look at the big serving-dish, as the young wife puts it on the table. But the food is great—just like mama makes it! *His* mama of course.

The commercial ends: 'You don't have to be Italian to cook like one. Not when you've got Hunt's tomato paste!' It gets through to us because we are involved.

Big organisations are finding out that it is good business to be personal in their dealings with their customers. And when we see how they do it, we get more lessons in how to make contact with the other person.

British Airways, New York, use Robert Morley as their spokesman. He chats to TV viewers as if they are friends. 'British Airways is expecting you', he announced in 1975, 'for the two hundredth Anniversary of your Revolution. So do come home. All is forgiven.' If you are kept waiting on the telephone, Robert Morley's voice tells you that he's sorry, but can you be patient for just a bit and they'll be right with you. If you're still waiting five minutes later:

> Still there, are you? Bravo. I wish I could give you a prize for endurance. Very soon now I am sure you are going to get your reservation call—and have a lovely time.

33

Frank Borman, the former astronaut, is president of Eastern Airlines and does his own TV commercials, so that he can talk to passengers. 'An Eastern plane is late,' he says, 'and that really bothers me . . . We'll accept good reasons for being late—but not bad ones . . . And neither will you. So most of the time we'll be on time.' Eastern Airlines' passengers feel involved and Eastern does well out of it.

From million-dollar advertising campaigns we come back across the Atlantic to a young photographer who is promoting her one-woman show of photographs in Cambridge, England. She wants publishers and critics from London to come to the private view. The first draft of her letter began:

> I am enclosing an invitation to the Private View on the 3rd November of my exhibition in Cambridge, and hope you might be able to attend.

Then she had second thoughts. Cambridge is about sixty miles from London and she was asking people to turn out on a cold and misty November evening. So she tried again, putting herself in the place of the person receiving her letter:

> I know Cambridge is nearly an hour and a half from London and that November evenings aren't inviting. But full of hope, I'm sending you an invitation to the Private View of my exhibition on the 3rd November. Please try to come.
>
> We'd make you very welcome and there will of course be drinks on hand.

By admitting that she was asking people to put themselves out, she won sympathy and a good attendance at the opening of her show.

The secretary of the Writers' Guild of Great Britain did the same thing when she recently asked members to complete a long questionnaire:

> I know you are very busy and that filling in forms is not the most attractive way to spend time, but if you could find time to give us your views the Committee and I would very much appreciate it.

As a result many members responded—including me. When

you see something as someone else will see it, you have gone towards them and are nearer to shaking hands.

An older woman decided, after bringing up her family, to take a training course in order to go back to work again. She is intelligent and has a lot to offer an employer. She began her letter of application:

> By the end of this month, I shall have completed a comprehensive business and commercial course at a College of Further Education. This full-time course has covered accountancy, commerce, secretarial duties and typewriting, including some audio work.

She sent out twenty letters but none led to an interview. I suggested that she considered what it's like to be the director or personnel manager who would read her letter. When she had worked up some sympathy for him, she wrote another letter. It began:

> Can you use in your business a woman who will be loyal, hard-working and reliable? I think I can offer you those qualities and also really up-to-date training, because I am just finishing a comprehensive business and commercial course at a College of Further Education.

Her next six letters led to four interviews.

Even when we are just explaining something, it helps to put ourselves in the other person's place. It's one thing to have something in our own mind: it's another thing to get it into someone else's.

You know what happens when you wind down the car window and ask the way. You can be treated to a torrent of second turnings on left, third lots of traffic lights and turn rights at T-junctions. 'Thank you very much', you say. And the moment he's gone, you turn to your passenger and ask 'What did he say?' Whoever was telling you the way did not put himself in the position of a 'stranger in those parts'.

Seeing things only our way produces breakdowns in communication even at the highest levels. Professor A. H. Halsey, the Oxford sociologist, tells us that international conferences are often farces of misunderstanding.

35

When we fail to get a message across, it is a failure of our imagination. Professor Bernard Williams of Cambridge, who is interested in linguistic philosophy, takes this line:

> We have a responsibility to make our words express what we mean, because we do not have these meanings inside us, independent of what we say. Our sentences *are* our meanings.

Unless we try to see things as the other person will see them, the shutters will come down and instead of communicating, we end up talking to ourselves.

On a hot summer's day, somewhere in England on a village cricket green, an enthusiastic schoolboy explained the rules of cricket to an American who had never seen the game before:

> One side is out in the field—the other side is in. Each man on the side that's in goes out and when he is out he comes in and the next man goes in until he's out.
>
> When they are all out, the side that's been out in the field comes in and the side that's been in goes out—and tries to get out those coming in.
>
> Is that quite clear, Sir?

As you approach Hemel Hempstead, Hertfordshire, there is a long steep hill with a big roundabout at the bottom. But this roundabout is *two-way* and you can turn either left or right. Most drivers have never met one like it before. When it was first set up like that, there was a sign: EXPERIMENTAL ROUNDABOUT AHEAD. But as they reached it, driver after driver goggled in disbelief and dismay at seeing traffic criss-crossing in both directions.

Nobody had considered what it was like to be a driver who expects roundabouts to be one-way systems. Even traffic signs can pass on information as if from one human being to another, as they did in Sydney, Australia when a two-way road was changed to one-way only. Any driver who didn't notice saw this sign:

GO BACK
you are going the
WRONG WAY

Carl Gustav Jung, the Swiss psychologist, has taught us more about ourselves than possibly any other man this century. But his books and papers are difficult to follow without psychological training. Not long before his death, Jung agreed to edit a book explaining his theories to people without much knowledge of psychology. Because he knew that this would be difficult, he made it a condition that John Freeman, the television interviewer and former ambassador, should be the co-ordinating editor of the book.

John Freeman tells how he was rather flattered when the great man chose him. But he didn't feel so pleased when he found that it was because Jung thought of him as being of reasonable, but not exceptional intelligence—anything John Freeman could understand could also be understood by the average reader.

Jung's approach worked: the book, *Man and His Symbols*, has introduced his teachings to many people.

We often have to consider how other people might understand something and the speed at which they can take it in. If you are a doctor talking to other doctors about the digestive tract, you can go along at a fair gallop. To explain the same thing to an anxious patient, you have to break it down into easily understood facts.

It is a common mistake to transmit information too quickly; we are often afraid of boring people if we slow down. Yet we know from our own experience how quickly we lose interest when we can't follow something. Next time you hear a speaker going too fast, look at the faces of the people around you and you'll see their attention slipping away. With a good speaker, notice his pace and rhythm and how he speaks slowly enough and clearly enough, in short neat phrases that everyone can take in, without having to work hard.

That is a good approach to using the telephone, which can be a strangely uneasy means of communication. It is intimate because someone is speaking right into our ear and we are doing the same to them: it is also distant, because they are not there

37

beside us. Some people like it, some don't. Most of us hang up at times feeling we have not said what we wanted in the way that we wanted to.

The telephone is used more and more now as a sales tool because of the high cost of personal selling. Some people find it difficult to be at ease talking to a stranger. A girl in New York has to phone about fifty people every evening and offer them a free dancing lesson. Every time she heard the *burr . . . burr* of the bell, she used to tense up because she was afraid of being snubbed.

Then she tried propping up by the phone a photograph of a man and woman she knows. As she looks at it, she finds her conversation flows more easily and her voice is relaxed. This used to be taught to early radio broadcasters to give them the feeling of person to person contact.

There is no need to use a photograph. When you are phoning someone you know, flash into your mind a mental picture of them talking back to you. If it's a stranger, use a mental image of someone you know. It is worth trying, because it has helped other people to be more natural and effective on the telephone.

Listen in on this conversation that I wrote down when I was allowed to spend an hour plugged in to a busy switchboard:

Operator	County Council Offices.
Caller	Give me Mr Cox, will you?
Operator	Do you know his extension, Sir?
Caller	It's your job to know that.
Operator	We've got over five hundred extensions here.
Caller	I can't help that. Just look it up.
Operator	Just a moment then.
Caller	Look operator, I'm in a hurry.
Operator	I'm doing my best, Sir.

A few seconds later

Operator	He's not answering.
Caller	Well where is he?
Operator	I don't know, Sir.
Caller	Can't you try another office?

At that point the operator pulled out the plug.

Luckily we do not all speak to telephone operators like that, or nobody would get through to anybody. Even on the telephone, maybe especially on the telephone, our words work better when we talk as one human being making contact with another.

What is called the 'passive voice' is bad for communication, because it is impersonal. It is the passive voice when you turn sentences round and say 'Your order has been received' instead of 'We've received your order', or 'Every attempt should be made by you' instead of 'You should go on trying', or 'The information you requested has been ascertained' instead of 'We have found out what you want to know'.

'It is felt', 'it is regretted', 'it is appreciated' are all signs of the passive voice. What is called 'white paper blindness' can lead us into this—we cannot see the other person. If we do turn our thoughts round in that way, we drive a wedge between us and whoever is reading our letters or reports. When we are talking to a friend, we use 'I' and 'you' all the time. 'It' is for objects and not for people.

'You are loved by me' will never do the same job as 'I love you'. As Jung said, words 'gain life and meaning only when you take into account their relationship to the living individual'.

Mervyn Stockwood, Bishop of Southwark, agrees with that. When he was vicar in a tough district of Bristol, he was looking through a draft of his curate's sermon. 'What does this mean to Charlie Hodder?' he boomed out. The Bishop explained to me that Charlie Hodder weighed about twenty stone, worked on the railways and 'had two places of worship—the church and the pub'.

Someone else once said to me that communication is like speaking on the telephone when it's a bad line and we have to get through all the crackles and splutters. That's how it is when we are talking or writing to someone. We have to do our best to get through all the fears, doubts, uncertainties and hang-ups that come between us and the other person.

39

It doesn't matter how good we are at using words and stringing them into sentences. That is not enough on its own— 'You've gotta have heart!'

4 Getting attention first

For thousands of years fables have been used to teach un-changing truths about human nature. Here is a fable about communication. The vital truth it contains can help us every time we use words.

It started as an old Russian story with a moral. Since then it has come up as a tale told by wiseacres in the United States. The truth behind it is universal and timeless and it could have been told anywhere at any time.

In a remote region of eastern Russia, there was a travelling wizard who could work wonders at training the most difficult of donkeys. They said all he had to do was to talk to the donkey and thenceforth it would obey every order. The wizard went from village to village selling his services.

In one village a peasant had a donkey whose obstinacy knew no bounds. The villagers believed it was a direct descendant of the original stubborn mule. The moment it was loaded up, it would sit down and refuse to respond to threats, beating or cajoling. Even when its owner dangled a carrot in front of its nose, the donkey wouldn't budge. Time and again the peasant had to unload it, curse his luck and carry the stuff on his own back.

When the wizard arrived in that village, you can guess who was the first in the queue. They agreed terms quickly, for the peasant was in no mood to haggle. The wizard began by walking slowly round the animal, examining it carefully. Everyone watched. After giving the matter some thought, the stranger rummaged in his bag, took out a large wooden mallet, advanced on the donkey and without hesitation smote it smartly between the eyes.

'I don't want him killed!' protested the owner, 'I heard that all you have to do is to talk to him.'

'Then you heard right, my friend,' replied the wizard. 'But you must understand something else—I have to get his attention first.'

Has this ever happened to you? You have gone to see your doctor, a solicitor or the chairman about something that really matters. After a while you become aware that he has something else on his mind. You see it in the lack of concentration in his eyes and hear it in the mechanical way he asks or answers questions. Most of us have been through this and have come away with a deep sense of dissatisfaction. We could not get across what we wanted to say.

At the same time, we know that when we ourselves are listening to someone, or reading a letter or report, our minds can be full of other things. Try the experiment of stopping and listening to the almost constant talk going on in your head. Total concentration is so rare that it is said it can work miracles.

If we all gave each other our undivided attention, our response would be alive and immediate. When we talk to our friends and family, there would be a heightened awareness of one another and every moment would count. But people will not often listen to us or read our words with so much attention. There are too many other things going on inside them. What can we do about this when it is important to get through to someone?

We can start by raising the level of attention they will give to what we are saying or writing. If we lift attention from twenty per cent to forty per cent, we have doubled it. And that can make all the difference.

Let's see this in action. These are actual examples of the beginnings of letters waiting on a sales manager's desk 9.30 one Monday morning:

Can we draw your attention to a new scheme for . . .
Our representative would like to call on you to discuss . . .
We understand that you might be interested in . . .
In reply to your letter of the 3rd July, enquiring about . . .

He goes through the letters quickly, puts some on one side to be

42

dealt with later and drops others into the wpb. In his office nothing stirs. The level of his attention is as flat as the water of a lake on a windless day.

Stifling a yawn, he plods on:

We are in receipt of your letter of the 30th August in connection with . . .

If your work involves travelling and entertainment, can we offer you unique Credit Card facilities?

We have 200 new ideas for putting punch into direct mail shots and promotion campaigns.

Good morning. I'm afraid it could be *Monday* morning. Just my luck! But that was a chance I had to take. You see, your enquiry arrived on Friday, and because we would very much like to have you as a customer, I dealt with it the same day.

Different people are turned on or put off by different things. But the way that last letter began caught the sales manager's attention. He read it twice and telephoned the writer to make an appointment. When I asked him why, he thought for a moment and then said, 'I suppose because it was different. It kinda woke me up a bit.'

Mary Wells Lawrence is the chairwoman of a successful advertising agency on Fifth Avenue, New York and is believed to be the highest paid woman executive in America. She says something very simple about the one thing all her advertisements have in common:

They all shake things up a little bit. They look at the product or service with a fresh eye.

Whoever wrote the letter that got the sales manger going that Monday morning had learned to do the same thing. His letter did not begin in the expected way: it shook things up a little bit.

When television arrived everyone thought it was a fantastic advertising medium. But there was a catch. Television has become known as the goggle-box; it is so easy to look at without any real attention. A recent *Washington Post* poll shows that people watch TV for about twenty-two hours a week. They also talk at the same time, have their supper, read the paper or even doze off.

Advertising people know that unless they get attention in the first few seconds of a commercial, they are lost.

One classic commercial began with a chimpanzee ambling into an office. Viewers looked up—what's a chimp doing in an office? He was taking a document to the Xerox machine and making copies to show how simple it is. Twenty years later people still remember that commercial. Thousands and thousands of others are forgotten because they did not lift the level of our attention.

Another successful commercial used suspense. It's a foggy night, a woman is driving on her own and she has a flat tyre. Everyone stopped talking and looked. What's going to happen? No problem. She drove on because her Goodyear tyres had built-in safety-spares.

The prize-winning Pozidriv commercial used involvement. Pozidriv screws do not have the usual slot in the head. This needed explanation: viewers would have to pay attention. The commercial started with a man screwing home an ordinary slotted screw. The screwdriver slips and scores a nicely polished surface. Everyone who has ever driven home a screw was immediately involved. Research showed that viewers looked at and listened to what came next.

The unexpected, suspense and involvement are three good ways of lifting the level of anyone's attention. Test them for yourself. The moment you see or read something unusual or a picture or headline connects with your own experience, or something makes you want to know what will happen next, your attention is caught. For the next few minutes you watch the screen or read the paper in a different way. If that happens to you, it also happens to everyone you communicate with.

A woman was getting a divorce. There were many complications and she was confused and worried. She wrote to her solicitor. At the end of the day he picked out her letter as the one that had stayed most in his mind. This was the first paragraph:

44

I know this is just one of many cases to you. But it is different for me. It's my divorce and the only one I'll ever have, I hope. My whole future depends upon whether it goes well. So please give me the best advice you can.

'How did that affect you?' I asked him.

'It made me stop and think,' he answered. 'It's not the way people usually write to their solicitors.'

'Did it make any difference to how you dealt with her case?' He hesitated. 'I do my best for every client.'

'But?' I asked.

He smiled. 'I didn't say *but*. But . . .' We both laughed.

'You know how it is—we're all human. And whatever you're doing, you can put a little extra into it.'

I agreed: 'None of us can function at peak level all the time.'

It would have been unfair to have pushed the point further. Solicitors, like doctors, surgeons and airline pilots, are supposed to give their best all the time. But who can do that? If something unexpected comes in, we sharpen our minds. We should all like to get that kind of attention when we write or say anything that could make a difference to our lives.

Any nut-case can get attention by doing something silly or shocking, or by promising something they cannot deliver. That's not good enough. People walk away when they find they've been tricked into gathering round.

Do all those calendars in cheap colour, with naked girls in coy poses, do anything more than make garage mechanics, from Sidcup to Solihull, New Haven to New Orleans, lust after lovely blondes, brunettes and redheads? Even Pirelli, whose calendars became collectors' pieces, got out of it: it is often said they were becoming better known for calendars than tyres.

When the client of an ad agency demanded record attention figures for his ads, the agency boss suggested: 'Instead of showing a big picture of the car you show a big picture of Marilyn Monroe and a little picture of the car. If that doesn't work, you take some clothes off her.'

A letter to young executives made a similar mistake. It began:

45

> What could you do with £35,000 hard cash? A new car, a new house, a long holiday. Why not make out your own list right now?

It got attention at the start. Then it went on to describe an insurance policy. If you are under thirty and pay so much a month for thirty-five years, that's the sum you might end up with. It was a let-down after the opening, which promised something just around the corner, not thirty-five years away.

If you trick people into giving you their attention, there is always the risk of backlash. They might reject everything that follows. It is more intelligent to raise the level of someone's attention in a way that relates directly to what you want them to know. The man who wrote to the sales manager could have gone too far:

> Good morning. I'm afraid that it could be *Monday* morning. And we all know what Monday mornings are like. You have a nice weekend, play golf, see your friends. And then Bang! It's Monday morning again, and here you are driving the car or catching the train to the office. The party's over.

That leads up the wrong alley. The sales manager would have had to read too much and then drag himself back to the point of the letter. As it was, he remembered the letter arrived on Monday because his enquiry had been received on Friday and had been dealt with the same day. He liked that.

In the States clever visual ideas on television, which draw attention away from the product advertised, are called video vampires. A few years back Brigitte Bardot suddenly appeared in a TV commercial. She had never made one before so signing her up was a coup. As you would expect, it wasn't cheap: a Sunday paper said the whole project cost half a million pounds.

Brigitte Bardot is not a vampire or even a vamp (the second word derives from the first). But in a discussion about this commercial recently, we all remembered seeing Bardot looking relaxed and lovely, but could not recall what she was advertising. Our own reaction doesn't prove anything; but there is always a risk of a clever idea stealing the show. An experienced politician once warned a young Member of Parliament, who was drafting his maiden speech, 'Don't let the idea upstage the message'.

When you are writing a letter, picking up the phone or going in to talk to someone, you have an advantage over every advertiser, even if he has a million pounds to spend. You are communicating with one person; you know their name or can often find it out; you know something about them and can sometimes find out more. Your first sentence can have an immediate relevance for that one person and the relationship between you. Compared to that, no matter how much research an advertiser does, he is putting a message in a bottle, hoping that the right person will find it, open it and read it.

I heard a friend make a telephone call to a big department store about a refrigerator that had not been delivered on time. Her old refrigerator had been sold to make space for the new one. It was summer and a heat-wave, so she had problems. This was her side of the conversation. She was speaking to the telephone operator to begin with:

> Do you know, or could you find out please, who deals with deliveries to customers in the London area?
>
> Thank you very much. Do you know his first name? . . . And his extension? . . . Thank you. It's really very friendly of you to help me like that. Would you put me through to him please?
>
> Is that Philip Elliott? . . . Oh good. My name is Mary Wilcox. I'm so glad to speak to you, because you're the one person who can help me. Isn't it lovely hot weather?
>
> I agree. It's marvellous! But would you believe it? I haven't got a refrigerator.

She went on to give him the essential details of her order.

Put that beside the usual approach:

> Hallo. Despatch department? I want to make an enquiry about a refrigerator that hasn't been delivered.

My friend started off by finding out the name of the actual man who could help her. She got his attention from the start by showing that she knew his name—'Is that Philip Elliott?' She followed up with the Kitchener-Needs-You approach: 'You're the one person who can help me'. And she went on from there.

I was tempted to go round to the store, find Philip Elliott and ask what effect that phone call had on him. But as it is results that count, I asked my friend to let me know when her refrigerator turned up. She telephoned the next day and invited me round for iced coffee.

When you are thinking of the best way to get attention in a letter, at a meeting or in any other communication, it is usually best to look first at the simple and direct way, even if it seems obvious. In 1975 Margaret Thatcher became the leader of the Conservative Party in Great Britain. This was the biggest landmark in the history of equality for women since they won the vote in 1928; it led to her becoming the first woman Prime Minister of Great Britain.

Soon afterwards, the Conservatives had a party political broadcast on television. Political broadcasts are not usually compulsive viewing. People have heard it all before. But here was a real chance to get everyone's attention from the start: the Conservative Party had a star attraction, the first woman in the Western world who was in line to become Prime Minister.

All it needed was for Margaret Thatcher to be there on the screen and we'd have been all eyes and ears. That was the simple way to do it and couldn't fail. What happened instead? The party political broadcast opened with a man.

Simple beginnings give us a much better chance to get to the heart of the matter:

Good morning. I'm afraid it could be *Monday* morning . . .

I know this is just one of many cases to you. But it is different for me . . .

. . . you're the one person who can help me.

Headlines teach us a lot about how to get attention with simplicity and directness. At their worst, they are confusing unless you think about them. And nobody bothers to do that. When you have to explain a headline, it's like having to explain a joke—you've failed. Good headlines say it all in a clear neat and memorable way.

Peter Hobden, an experienced advertising writer, was working with a designer on ideas to put over a new breakthrough for London transport. Instead of the tedious journey by bus to Heathrow, London's main airport, passengers could now take an underground train all the way from the centre of London. The designer was doodling, the way designers do when they are hunting around for ideas, and he sketched an underground train with the nose of an aircraft at the front. Something clicked and Peter Hobden wrote:

FLY THE TUBE!

The news, the excitement, the speed and the convenience were all there in three short words.

Most pens are shiny. Parker produced a matt black pen. It looked more distinguished, in the way that the soft sheen of stainless steel looks more distinguished than chromium. The advertising agency had to say that in a few words on a small poster, in a way that gave the pen distinction, took full advantage of the reputation behind the name Parker and caught our attention. Their solution was:

ONLY PARKER CAN MAKE A PEN THAT DULL

Here are some other headlines that have stopped people:

WE DON'T THINK PEOPLE SHOULD MAKE MONEY OUT OF ABORTION

(For a pregnancy advisory service)

WE'RE RICH! JOIN US!

(For a newsletter to help investors)

DON'T GIVE THE GIFT THAT GOES ON GIVING

(For a VD clinic in Berkeley, California)

THE MOST WORTHWHILE WEEKEND OF YOUR LIFE?

(For a week-end course, at the Manchester Business School, for people who want to start new businesses)

49

LE CRUNCH—FRENCH GOLDEN DELICIOUS APPLES
(On a barrow of fruit)

Those headlines have one thing in common: they are simple, direct and make a relationship between us and what they are saying.

We cannot always think of a clever idea. But we can always start with something simple. This is Sir Richard Steele beginning a letter to his wife, when he was away from home on 30 September 1710:

> I am very sleepy and tired, but could not think of closing my eyes till I had told you I am, dearest creature, your most affectionate and faithful husband.

This is a seventeen-year-old boy answering the first question at an interview:

> No I don't have any experience, sir. I've just left school. But if you give me the job, I'll be as intelligent as I can and work as hard as I can.

This is the beginning of a letter from a woman replying to a final notice to pay an overdue account:

> I will pay the bill. I promise you that. But I can't pay it right away. The reasons don't matter, and would only bore you. Please can I have another month? That's all I need.

Advertising experts say a headline that asks a question is a guaranteed way of attracting attention. It can also work at the beginning of letters, of meetings and even in a poem.

The most arresting first line of any poem was a question by John Donne, the seventeenth-century mystical poet:

> What if this present were the world's last night?

When winter was getting under way, this question was at the top of an advertisement:

WHAT WILL YOU DO TOMORROW IF THE CAR WON'T START?

That can also seem like the end of the world. It was an advertisement for an anti-damp spray.

Orbach's, the store in New York that sells women's clothes at cheap prices, hooked the attention of every woman by asking:

DOES YOUR BABY-SITTER LOOK BETTER
COMING IN THAN YOU DO GOING OUT?

A successful letter to local firms used a question as the first sentence:

> Would an experienced, fast and reliable local office cleaning service save you a lot of trouble?

A small company was in an ugly situation because of labour troubles. The managing director went to a meeting with the staff. He began with a question: 'Please can we start off by asking: What is the one thing we all want?' The question made everyone stop and think. If each side wanted something different, there could only be an impasse. But if both sides wanted to get back to work, there was a chance.

Personal and human opening sentences attract attention. Book titles show how: one writer changed 'It Was Always Hot' to *Some Like It Hot*; 'The Witch' became *I Married a Witch*; 'The Lost Wife' was changed to *The Man Who Lost His Wife*.

Instead of starting, as one letter did, 'It is important to have up-to-date information about export markets.' we could say, 'A managing director wanted to be right up-to-date about export markets.' That gets more attention because it is more personal.

When you use an unexpected approach, you will often be met with 'You can't say things like that'. Don't always listen. Rosie is a copywriter in a big ad agency. Her husband has his own business and she does some typing for him in the evening. She has a lively sense of good communication and often re-writes the beginnings of his letters. In one case, she changed:

> We acknowledge receipt of your first order, but regret that we are unable to deliver by the date specified. The 27th June is the earliest we can manage.

to:

> We were so glad to get your order and welcome you as a new customer. We hate saying we can't make your delivery date. Can

51

you possibly wait until the 27th June? If you can, we'll bust a gut to get it to you by then.

'You can't say things like that,' her husband said.

'Why not?'

'Because people don't write like that in business letters. That's why.'

'What's so special about a business letter already? It's just one person talking to another.'

With people we are very close to, perhaps especially with those we love, we have to find ways sometimes to lift the level of attention, or a marvellous moment would be lost. Thornton Wilder, the American playwright, captured this in his play *Our Town*. Emily, the daughter of the family, dies in childbirth at twenty-seven. She is allowed back to live one day over again, but she has to watch herself reliving it. She chooses her fourteenth birthday.

As she goes through the morning of that day, she alone knows how little time she has left and she cannot bear the way no one is looking or listening with any real attention. It is all going so fast. She cries out: 'Oh, Mama, just look at me one minute as though you really saw me.'

A father took his twelve-year-old son outside to look at an eclipse of the sun. After a few moments, he clouted the boy round the head. 'I'm sorry, Mike. But I want you to wake up and *look*—then you'll remember seeing it for the rest of your life.'

Research has shown that people in cities come up against some sixteen hundred advertising messages each day. How anyone works out that kind of figure is not clear, but just accept it. Add the thousands of other impressions made on us from the moment we get out of bed in the morning. Now add to the total those thoughts, feelings, fears and emotions churning around inside us. When we want to get attention from someone—all that is the competition.

As long ago as 1710, when life was much quieter and simpler, Steele and Addison gave this advice in *The Tatler*: 'The great

art in writing advertisements is to catch the reader's eye.'
Albert D. Lasker, one of the great masters of American advertising, put it with more punch—'You must stop the streetcar
before you get on it.'

5 On not boring the pants off them

When we bore someone all communication breaks down. The other person switches off and stops listening or reading. It doesn't matter if it's a friend, our husband, our wife, a customer or the chairman, if we bore them they are no longer with us. From that point on we are wasting our time.

Read this classified advertisement, perhaps the most famous one that ever appeared:

> MEN WANTED for Hazardous Journey. Small wages, bitter cold, long months of complete darkness, constant danger, safe return doubtful. Honour and recognition in case of success.

It is part of the documentation of Ernest Shackleton's expedition to the South Pole. The words are uninviting and flat: they offer little and promise nothing. Yet the response was overwhelming.

What attracted people? In spite of the hardship and the danger, perhaps because of them, the journey must have seemed like an antidote to boredom. And people will do almost anything to escape being bored.

Boredom is like an illness. When we are bored life drags. Nothing tastes any good or looks any good. It follows that the last thing we want is to bore someone, because no communication can succeed if it does that.

What happens when you listen to someone talking and it's uninteresting? It can feel like crossing a desert without an oasis in sight. When you read something that doesn't interest you, you don't go on with it, unless you have to. Then it's a struggle. You can imagine you are tired, hungry or even ill—anything that gives you an excuse to stop reading.

Suppose you are the one who is boring someone. How does it

feel as the flow of communication peters out? These three situations actually took place:

Case 1
A salesman is with a director of a company, selling him a delivery service for the London area. He talks about the number of messengers they have available on motorbikes, shows him a list of firms who employ them, explains the radio call links and how they are organised.

It is quite impressive. But he comes away saying, 'It was no good—he just didn't want to know.' The other man was polite but bored. And that's the death of a salesman.

Case 2
The principal of a New York advertising agency is explaining to the president of a big company the reorganisation of the agency's creative departments.

After a while, the president gets up and says, 'I couldn't be less interested in the saga of your company.'

Case 3
A secretary is talking to her boss about her salary. She explains how her fares have gone up, how much she has to pay for lunch and that she is feeling left behind generally in the rates of pay for secretaries.

Her boss looks at his watch and says, 'You'll have to excuse me, Sally, but I've got a meeting in a couple of minutes.'

The salesman, the head of the ad agency and Sally all made the same mistake: they did not take into account the limit of interest operating in the other person. Just as our own time and interest are usually limited, so is everyone else's. The moment we go beyond someone's limit of interest, we start to lose contact. This explains why every year millions of pounds of communication are wasted.

Research has shown that if you take a half-page advertisement in a national daily paper, about twenty per cent of readers will not even look at the page; fifty per cent look at the page but not at the advertisement; that leaves thirty per cent who look at the ad—and only some of those read it. Boring people can cost a lot of money.

Government departments send out forms with whole pages packed with instructions. The result: millions of forms are filled in wrongly or not filled in at all. 'Life', as the old song goes, 'gets tedious—don't it?'

The way to keep any communication in any form alive and interesting to the other person is to keep within their limit of interest or find a way to extend it. Because a limit of interest is not fixed: it always depends upon the involvement of one person with the other or with the subject. When something is about us, our limit of interest expands generously. 'Talk to me about *me*', as the pretty blonde said when she was asked, 'What shall we talk about?'

We extend someone's limit of interest by turning round what we are saying or writing so that we talk about them. Let's try this out in our three case histories:

Case 1
The unsuccessful salesman could have asked, 'Do you know how many of your firm's letters are sent to the London area? Generally it's at least fifty per cent. How would you like to be sure that nearly all those letters are delivered the same day at no more cost than first-class postage?'

Case 2
The principal of the New York ad agency would not have bored his client if he had said, 'I thought you would like to know we can now put more creative man hours into your advertising without it costing you a cent more.'

Case 3
Sally would have stood a much better chance of getting through if she had said to her boss, 'I know you're under pressure and need all the help you can get. Will you help me to go on doing my best for you?'

The need to talk about ourselves is so strong that it works as a therapy. A wise family doctor knows that if he talks to patients about themselves, it often does them more good than medicine. When the BBC did a series of radio programmes on psychotherapy, they called it 'Let's talk about me'.

At the beginning of her novel *Persuasion*, Jane Austen describes how Sir Walter Elliot only ever picked up one book, which was the list of Baronets. It always fell open at the same page:

ELLIOT OF KELLYNCH HALL
Walter Elliot, born March 1, 1760, married July 15 1784, Elizabeth, daughter of James Stevenson Esq. of South Park in the county of Gloucester; by which lady (who died 1800) he has issue, Elizabeth, born June 1, 1785; Anne, born August 9, 1787; a still-born son, November 5, 1789; Mary, born November 20, 1791.

If all that took you beyond your limit of interest, please forgive me. It was to make a point. For Sir Walter Elliot that was fascinating stuff and he could read it and re-read it 'with an interest which never failed'.

It's like a bad joke in the advertising business when a client wants to show in his ads a picture of the new factory; and to tell everyone how big it is, how many people work there and all the rest of the things he is proud of. The result, for other people, would be one big yawn.

When Ford, in the US, were looking for a name for their new car, more than six thousand were submitted. Their ad agency listed Corsair, Ranger and Pacer as the top three suggestions. Ford chose *Edsel*, the first name of Henry Ford I. But it didn't mean much to anyone else. The Edsel was the biggest failure in marketing history.

Ruth Waldo, a group head with J. Walter Thompson, the biggest ad agency in the world, warns against copywriters seeing too much of clients because 'they begin thinking about Mr X as the client rather than about the people who buy the product'.

Whenever we write business letters, sales letters, letters to help someone; or when we go into a meeting, deliver a Sunday morning sermon, pick up the phone to speak to a customer or a friend, it always helps to remember what happens when a manufacturer shows a picture of his own factory: nobody wants to know.

This advertisement for a second-hand car appeared in a local paper:

£700 is dear for a 14-year-old VW. But it's cheap if you want the feeling of driving a VW that's done only 25,000 miles and looks *three* years old.

That is interesting because it puts us in the driving seat. Compare it to this letter:

We are glad to tell you about the success of our new car-leasing facilities. In the last year, over 700 cars have been leased through us for the directors and executives of well-known companies. These include . . .

Or this one:

When it comes to office furniture, no one can give you a bigger choice than we can. We have been in the business for fifty years, and we are proud of our Showrooms with their four floors of desks and chairs waiting for you to inspect.

As Managing Director, I should like to add . . .

Those two letters, in their own way, are just showing a picture of the factory.

The surest of all ways to bore people is to write or say too much—we run out of interest the way sand runs through an egg-timer. Check your reaction next time a long letter or report lands on your desk or doormat. Most of us recoil from the effort we have to make to get through it.

Everyone has too much to read: newspapers and trade magazines pile up, circulars and internal memos plop into in-trays. Put side by side these two letters from women who are replying to a stern letter from their bank manager:

Letter 1

I was horrified to get your letter and to find out the size of my overdraft. The trouble is I had been on holiday on the Costa Brava and had spent much more than I had intended. I'm sure you know what it's like when you go on holiday and just forget how much you are getting through.

Then when I got back, my Mini needed a MOT and that meant new brake linings and one or two other things, so the bill came to £125 which was much more than I could possibly have expected.

58

While I was on holiday, I broke a tooth, and had to have a gold crown fitted and that came to £60 which I'm sure you'll agree is a lot of money to have to find suddenly.

And that was not the end of it.

Letter 2
Thank you for warning me that I am so much overdrawn. Several emergencies all came together. I'm sorry, because I should have asked you first.
    Everything is all right now. I'll be able to clear the overdraft within three months by going carefully.

This was the bank manager's reaction. *Letter 2* gave him confidence in the reliability of his customer and he continued to allow her a small overdraft.

The length of what we write or say must relate to the reader's or listener's limit of interest, or our communication will fall as flat as a pancake. If we are going to buy a new car, we're usually willing to read a lot about it. Specialists have a high limit of interest about any new developments in their field. But remember even experts are sometimes bored out of their minds at conventions and conferences, listening to long papers read by other experts who are carried away by their own knowledge and enthusiasm.

It is different with literature. If you want to write a novel as long as *War and Peace* (about 600,000 words) go ahead. But you'll find most publishers are much happier with 60,000 words, because they're in business to sell books.

It is different also with legal documents when you have to use recognised standard phrases to be as clear and precise as language will allow. This is a special area and length is not so important, although I like the story a young solicitor told against himself. He had gone with his client for a meeting with a busy QC. The QC opened the meeting by saying that he had had time to read only half the brief.

'But that won't do at all.' protested the solicitor, 'All the important matters are covered in the second half.'

'That was the half I read,' replied the counsel.

When Johan Gutenburg set up around 1450 the first printing press using movable type, he started something. For the next five hundred years the printed word was the most effective way of influencing the greatest number of people. Through words in print, revolutions were brought about, governments overturned and social orders challenged. That age has come to an end.

Now most people take in most of their information from pictures. The washing instructions on your shirt or skirt and the markings on the knobs and levers on your car are symbols, not words. And you don't have to read any more to find the right loo: an outline figure tells you which door.

We are all used to an electronic immediacy and can get impatient if there are too many words. Brevity is a marvellous quality in communication and the best way to avoid boring people.

The ancient Greeks were true to this principle and the great passages from their literature demonstrate it. Plato's comment on the death of his master, which saddened his whole life, was only a few words:

> Such was the death of our friend, the best man, I think, that I have ever known, the wisest too and the most just.

Churchill's economy of words was also marvellous and moving. In June 1940 the Germans occupied Paris and soon afterwards the French Government surrendered. Hitler boasted 'The war in the West is ended!' Churchill broadcast to the people of Britain. All he said was just over a hundred words:

> The news from France is very bad and I grieve for the gallant French people who have fallen into this terrible misfortune. Nothing will alter our feelings towards them or our faith that the genius of France will rise again. What has happened in France makes no difference to our actions and purpose. We have become the sole champions now in arms to defend the world cause. We shall do our best to be worthy of this high honour. We shall defend our island home and with the British Empire we shall fight on unconquerable until the curse of Hitler is lifted from the brows of mankind. We are sure that in the end all will come right.

When you want to make a letter or a report shorter, cutting out a word here and there makes hardly any difference and might change the feeling or meaning. Instead take out whole sentences and complete paragraphs. Rudyard Kipling believed that the main purpose of revision is deletion and that is a good rule to follow. When there are less of them, every one of our words does more work for us.

Anybody can make a mistake. But justifying ourselves is boring. Two examples from American television history show that people can respond to someone who goofs and admits it right away. The stories are true although precise details are difficult to establish.

In the days before videotape, a commercial for a cigarette lighter was going out 'live'. The actor flipped the lighter three times and it wouldn't work. A technician struck a match, leant in and said 'Would you like a *real* light?'

A famous programme host was demonstrating a refrigerator in a 'live' show. The new quick-release ice tray jammed and it took a lot of effort to yank it out. He held it up to the camera, saying, 'When they can make one that works, I'll tell you about it.'

It was a network show with high ratings and in the control room the man from the ad agency died a thousand deaths.

In those cases, sales of the cigarette lighter and of that make of refrigerator went up. Perhaps people responded to the direct acceptance that something had gone wrong. It is worth remembering this next time we make a mess of something. Long explanations and justifications rarely interest anyone and even judges, who are paid to listen to them, sometimes doze off.

We are all bored by a lot of facts and figures. Margaret Thatcher admitted that one of her speeches did not go well because 'it was too full of facts and figures. The next speech I made in the House was very successful—it had only a few facts and figures.'

A successful business consultant sends his clients a short letter, after he has looked into the problem. He says, 'This is what I advise you to do.' And he tells them. The supporting facts and figures are set out separately, so it is clear that all the homework has been done. He knows that his clients employ him more for his recommendations than anything else.

A young woman used this technique to save a long tedious discussion with her husband. After dinner one evening she said:

> I believe we ought to have a dish-washer. I don't want to bore you with all the reasons why. So I've written them out on this piece of paper in case you want to go through them. But if you don't want to, that's fine. Can I go out and order one tomorrow?

A letter or a report can *look* boring before we start to read it. And if we think we are going to be bored, our limit of interest drops a long way down. Before you send it out, hold up an important letter or report, not to see what it reads like, but to see what it looks like before anyone reads a word.

A lot of work goes into book-jackets and the packaging of a box of chocolates or a packet of cigarettes. It does not change the contents. But it does affect us and our immediate response. A letter can look efficient, reliable or friendly, just as a report can look easy to read.

When people are reading they often hear the words in their head. A letter can have a boring voice or it can sound full of energy and feeling. Short sentences, as well as being easier to understand, seem alert and vital. Compare this in a letter from a solicitor:

> It is considered advisable to bring to your attention that it cannot be assumed that the action will be successful, although you can be assured that nothing will be overlooked that could add to the strength of your case, and that our best efforts will be made on your behalf.

to this rewrite:

> You cannot be sure to win the action. But you can be sure that we'll use everything that is on your side. We promise to do our best for you.

Short words work better than long ones. English is rich in

monosyllables, much richer than most other languages, and when we use them our sentences zip along. Too many long words drag.

Some writers can make us interested in almost anything. Alistair Cooke describes how he sits down at his typewriter, says, 'Good evening', and goes on talking to the typewriter. We're usually happy to listen, because his easy free-association of one idea to the next takes us along with him all the way from his 'Good evening' to his 'Good night'. If you can do that, you might as well skip this chapter as you're not likely to bore the pants off anyone. A personal letter from the President of the United States also has a lot going for it.

The rest of us can adapt this advice from an expert on TV commercials: 'If you want to make thirty seconds seem a long time, don't do much in it.' Think of it this way: if you want to make your letters, reports and phone calls seem important, don't write or say too much.

Readership studies show that the less separate elements there are in an advertisement and the more they are brought together into one simple message, the more the advertisement will be read, remembered and acted on. Irving Berlin, who understood that, made a fortune, lost it in the Wall Street crash and made a second fortune. 'All I need', he said, 'is a catchy phrase that anyone can understand.' His songs never bored the pants off anyone:

There's no business like Show Business!
Oh how I hate to get up in the morning!
I'm dreaming of a white Christmas.
What'll I do when you are far away?
Isn't it a lovely day to be caught in the rain?

When people are talking they use a much smaller vocabulary than when they are writing. A journalist or novelist uses many more words in their work than in their conversation. If something you write sounds heavy-going, you can lighten it by looking at all those words you would not normally use in conversation. If some of them are not essential, change them to words you would say. Then read your letter again and see the difference.

There is a well-known bookshop in the Latin Quarter of Paris, where you queue first to give the book you have chosen to an assistant and get a bill. You leave the book behind and queue at the cash desk to pay. Then you come back and queue a third time, show the receipt to the assistant and take away your book. Buying a book in that shop is hard work.

Any communication can be a hassle like that. It can make you go backwards and forwards, trying to work it out. The most reliable rule for not boring anyone when you write or speak is to make it easy for them. They might have a lot of other things on their plate.

I should like to end this chapter with a salute to Roy Brooks, a London estate agent of the 1960s, who made boring lists of properties so *un*boring that thousands of people used to read them every week in the Sunday papers. Through them, he became the best known estate agent in the country. Here are three examples:

EARLS CT. Spacious 2nd/3rd flr Mais which fiercely bearded painter acquired 'from a rather dull fella in the Secret Service. I sculpt a bit in wood so I've been able to do some smashing fitted cupbds in kit.' Artistic arch links 2 rec rms to form fab STUDIO rec rm. 3 Bedrms. Bathrm. kit. steel sink unit. SUN-BATHING ROOF. Lse 64 yrs. GR £19 ONLY £6,995 even try an offer.

'I was a teenage literary agent' confessed Mrs L, gazing thro' the wall of glass in her new Nursery/Study, at the garden. 'A pity we had to cut the walnut tree down.' The rest is XVIIIth CENT. A small house of alleged royal ownership in the days of Kew Palace. On Kew Green & at rear looking to River and over Tennis Courts. An enchanting dble drawing rm, clkrm, and mod kit. 2 principal bedrms, small 3rd bedrm for child or dwarf lodger. All the class of living behind a Georgian fanlight for less than the price of a suburban villa. Only £8,995 FREEHOLD. View Sun.

There is a fashionable odour of decay in this PIMLICO PERIOD RES. 8/9 rms in horrible state of decoration. Innocent of all modern amenities. Mini mud patch at rear. Single family occupation only as subletting not allowed in this fashionable slum development. BARGAIN £8,450. Lse 80 yrs. G.R. £50. Key Brooks.

In case you are wondering whether they sold a lot of houses and flats, I can tell you because I asked: they did.

6 The way to give words added value

In economics 'added value' is doing something to raw material that makes it worth more. Virgin wool is dyed and woven into cloth, which adds value to it, more value still if people like the colour. Value is added to wine in casks by bottling it; and a good label adds even more value.

It is an exciting concept to think of words as the raw materials of communication. They acquire added value when they are put together in a way that makes people read them, listen to them, be inspired by them, moved by them or influenced by them.

It was said once that Webster's Dictionary contains all the words in the English language. That's not true, of course, not even for the thirteen heavy volumes of *The Oxford English Dictionary*. Words are all over the place and no one can ever find them all. But a small pocket dictionary gives you enough words to make language do anything for you. The moment you put some of those words into a simple phrase that has meaning for someone else, you have given them added value.

Good ideas add a lot of value to words: they take something ordinary and make it dramatic, new and alive. You can tell a girl that here is a hair-rinse that leaves your hair fair. An American advertising writer went a lot more than one better:

You've got only one life to live—so why not live it as a blonde?

Anyone can say the engine of a Rolls-Royce is so quiet you can hardly hear it. David Ogilvy, an Englishman who opened his own advertising agency in New York of all places, said it this way:

At 60 miles an hour the loudest noise in this new Rolls-Royce comes from the electric clock.

When with some pride he submitted the headline for approval, the senior Rolls-Royce executive resident in New York, 'that austere British engineer' as Ogilvy called him, hesitated for a moment or two and then said thoughtfully, 'We really must do something to improve our clock.'

The Walls Meat Company could have said their meat pies have a lot of meat in them. Someone had a better idea:

> Walls Meat Pies—Light on Pastry
> Heavy on Meat.

Avis are not the biggest in the car-hire business. A clever idea turned a negative into a plus, adding a lot of value to plain words— 'We're No. 2. So we try harder.' 'We try harder' became a catchphrase and doubled the Avis share of the car-hire business.

Remember this book a few years ago: *Everything You Always Wanted to Know About Sex but Were Afraid to Ask*? The last five words add the value. They link up with those unexpressed doubts and uncertainties that most of us feel about sex.

Poets add more value to words than anyone else, because their words can give us a new insight. No one knows how poetry works. It has something to do with the rhythm of the words, the choice of words or the use of an unexpected word that jolts our awareness. When W. H. Auden writes about being in bed and making love, the rhythm is quiet and reflective:

> Learn what love alone can teach:
> Happy on a tousled bed.

The unexpected word 'tousled' gives us a little shock of recognition and connects with our own experience.

John Tessimond, another poet, was an advertising copywriter, so when he writes about love, his words are simple. The added value comes from the rhythm and transparent sincerity:

> No more time or place
> Once I see her face.
> Sorrow, doubt and fear
> Leave when she is near.
> Warm, her eyes and hand,
> Wordless, understand.

Robert W. Bork, a Solicitor General of the United States, said, 'If people buy little daydreams with advertising, I don't know that we ought to be terribly upset about it.' John Tessimond, the poet, wrote advertising that added value to words in just that way. Here's one of his ads for shoes:

THE GIRL WHO WANTED THE MOON IN HER HAND

Once upon a time there was a girl
who had been invited to go dancing
one night in December.

Then, if never again, she wanted the
moon in her hand and the world at her
feet. The world and one man especially.

She found the dress in Paris, the
stockings, the perfume.

And the *shoes*? The shoes were in her
mind's eye. Light and slight as air.
slim and young and soft, white and
gold and gleaming.

We found her the shoes. Golden-
strapped, featherlight but firm.
Held firm by the fine spun strength
of white nylon mesh.

Shoes to dance in till dawn.

A lot of unknown, unsung people have given words added value by inventing catch-phrases. They present us 'free, gratis and for nothing' with an off-the-peg stock of good ways to give words the added value of sharpness and wit:

Hold your horses!
Let it all hang out.
Money for old rope.
It fell off the back of a lorry.
I wasn't born yesterday.
Run it up on the flagpole and see who salutes it.
Don't rock the boat!

And there are a whole lot more where they came from.

How can you give your own words added value? Not many of us have the intuition of a poet. And maybe you cannot snatch out of the clouds a great idea just when you want one. But there is a simple approach that can step up the value of words any time you want to use it.

Words always take on added value when they appeal to someone's motives and interests. When your words do that, they leap up in value. The first step is to think what the other person wants.

Some psychologists assert that if we peel back enough layers, we find our motive for doing anything is self-interest. But it is complex enough to try to penetrate the meaning of life without having such a large spanner thrown in the works. So there's no need to deny the existence of altruism, objective truth, beauty and form.

The day-to-day struggle in the jungle we live in is something else. Dr Edward de Bono, an expert on the processes of creative thinking, says without hesitation, 'In some form or another the pay-off is the reason for all action.' That's how it is a lot of the time in the world of letters, memos, meetings and telephone calls. If these are to be successful, we must be aware of the motives of the people we are dealing with. Then even the simplest words have added value.

When Guinness first started advertising in 1928, a couple of copywriters went from pub to pub, talking to Guinness drinkers. They kept finding people who thought Guinness did them good. That's what people wanted so that's what the copywriters said —as simply as possible:

GUINNESS IS GOOD FOR YOU

When drivers wanted speed and performance from petrol, rather than miles per gallon, Shell offered it to them in four easy words:

THAT'S SHELL—THAT WAS!

If something costs a lot of money people want it to last a long time. These words made that promise:

DIAMONDS ARE FOREVER

All the evidence and research I have ever seen shows that when it comes to adding value to words, simplicity leaves clever intellectual ideas miles behind.

We can get ideas from the ways advertising uses psychology and research to locate and define motives. Because an advertising campaign that makes the wrong appeal can waste millions, advertisers employ psychologists to probe deeper, below the rational obvious levels, down into the unconscious.

The American writer Vance Packard, whose book *The Hidden Persuaders* attacked the use of psycho-analysis by advertising agencies, reluctantly accepted:

> . . . that some pushing and hauling of the citizenry is probably necessary to make our $400,000,000,000-a-year economy work.

(That figure was quoted in 1957, by the way.) But he rejected the use of psycho-analysis to sell goods by using people's unconscious fears and anxieties.

Without going as far as that, some knowledge of how we function can make our communications with other human beings more valuable for us and to them. It is intelligent and reasonable to develop some awareness of motives and needs, so that we can give our words added value by making the right appeals instead of the wrong ones.

In the advertising business they call it motivational research. One technique is the depth-interview, a one-to-one meeting between a psychologist and someone who has volunteered to talk about why they buy certain products.

Not far from New York, six hundred feet up overlooking the Hudson River, was the Institute for Motivational Research. It is not an academic institute but a successful business that helps advertisers to understand their customers' motives. Other research companies sell different methods. There is a lot of disagreement even among the experts.

When the American Jesuits wanted to get more members, they turned to Dr Ernest Dichter, founder of the Institute for Motivational Research Inc. He told them, 'Don't offer them a

70

life after death, but a full and satisfying life on this earth—the same as industry.'

Dr Dichter, who early in his career was a psycho-analyst in that well-spring of psycho-analysis, Vienna, makes a great thing of the importance of emotional security in every sales approach. Another psychologist advises, 'If you want people to do something, you have got to help them feel right about doing it.'

Airlines have for a long time been interested in attitudes towards flying. Psychological research carried out by the University of London suggests that passengers in some way associate a flight with the idea of an operation in hospital. The pilot has the image of the surgeon, the man in charge. Stewardesses fit into the role of nurses. You can see how these unconscious connections could be made. When you enter an aircraft, you are to some extent helpless. From then on, other people are in charge and your life is at stake.

Manufacturers of cake-mixes also found they were getting into deep emotional stuff. A social psychologist advised them that a woman baking a cake makes some kind of a connection with the birth of a child. It is still said that a pregnant girl 'has a bun in the oven'. Cake-mix manufacturers have accepted that it is good for business to help women feel more creative by letting them add their own eggs or milk to the mixture.

Some of the conclusions of motivational research are bizarre. One famous expert admitted 'Sometimes, I think we can go in too deep'. We do not have to believe all of it. But some of the ideas are interesting and encourage us to go a little below the surface ourselves in our own attempts to understand how our words can get through.

The next time you write for a job, or ask a girl out to dinner, or a man home for a drink, there is no need to dive into the deep dark waters of depth-psychology. Down there even the experts get lost and confused. But most of us have the capacity, through understanding ourselves, to become more aware of the human psyche, that blend of emotional, intellectual and instinctive forces within us that make us respond, react, accept, reject, love and hate.

It may be comforting to think that we behave rationally, that we always know what we are doing and why we are doing it. But what is rational to you might not be rational to someone else. Our words start to take on added value from the moment we understand and accept that the other person will not automatically see things in the way we want them to.

Protagoras, an ancient Greek teacher, discovered that truth is not cut and dried. It depends on how we see it. Everything has to relate to man: 'Man is the measure of all things'. The Scottish psychiatrist, Dr R. D. Laing, believes that what society calls madness can be a perfectly clear and consistent view of life. It is just a completely different view from the one that most of us live with.

How can we make use of this when we put words together for something as practical as getting a complaint dealt with, putting up a recommendation to the board of directors or asking our wife or husband to accept that we don't want to go out this evening? We want our words to cross the gap between the way we see things and the way the other person sees them.

Suppose our heart is set on carrying through a new project and we want the go-ahead. The Board wants profit-margins increased, which requires more sales or lower costs. If we use our words to offer them what they want, we start to close the gap between us. Making words attractive to someone else is giving them added value.

It is not usually enough to give people the facts. We have to say how those facts offer them something they want. There is a world of difference between saying that apples contain vitamins and natural sugar and that inspired early marketing know-how 'An apple a day keeps the doctor away!'

Back in the early days of vacuum-cleaners, there was an unknown, long since forgotten door-to-door salesman who thought of taking with him on his calls a bag of dirt. He spread it on the carpet and let the housewife see the vacuum-cleaner suck it up. More than half a century later, advertising experts are paid a lot of money to advise that the most effective way to sell on television is to demonstrate. The old vacuum-cleaner salesman knew it from the seat of his pants. Demonstration takes the facts and shows what they will do for us.

An American commercial for Volkswagen showed an icy scene with a VW buried in a snow-drift. The announcer asks: 'How does the guy who drives the snow-plough get to the snow-plough?' A man gets into the Volkswagen, starts it up first time and drives off.

Another American commercial, for DieHard batteries, sold a lot of batteries by demonstrating that they live up to their name. Five cars, all with flat batteries, are started one after the other with the same two-year-old DieHard.

A girl used this principle to get a job in films. She wrote to a film producer offering to work a week for nothing to demonstrate that she is efficient, quick-thinking and reliable. He took her up on it. At the end of the week, he decided to pay her and give her the job.

Words can demonstrate things. A secretary wrote to me for a job and instead of saying her shorthand speed was 120 words a minute, she showed what it would do for me:

> You can dictate to me at two words a second, and when you see it typed out it will usually be accurate, word for word as you dictated it.

Everybody is selling something. Go to any meeting and you hear people selling ideas, theories, points of view or attitudes. Every high street is full of shop windows inviting us to buy. Every politician sells the advantages of electing him and his party. The Queen in her Christmas Day broadcast sells goodwill and national unity. Successful selling with words, as with demonstrations, starts with recognition of what the other person wants. Otherwise why should anyone listen to us?

A few years ago an international financier advertised for staff to sell his investment schemes, using the headline:

DO YOU SINCERELY WANT TO BE RICH?

It is probably true that money is the pay-off that attracts people more than any other. But it is a substitute for the things most of us really want, which are security, happiness and peace of mind. If you offer those things, they will always add value to your words.

It is normal to want to be liked. Generally people prefer to say *yes* rather than *no* and are often more willing to do something for us than we realise. Many times it makes little difference to them: it could mean nothing more than walking along to the next office and speaking to someone or picking up the phone and speaking to another department. People will often help if we ask in the right way.

Put yourself at the receiving end of the following two requests:

We are in a hurry for this so could you send it as soon as you can?

We are in a fix over this. And every day counts. Will you please do what you can to help us?

They both came in the same post addressed to a busy production manager. The second request got priority.

Making the right appeal is everything. I was asked to comment on this slogan for a road safety campaign:

TEACH YOUR CHILDREN THE GREEN KNIGHT
SAFETY RULES

I suggested something on these lines would offer more to parents:

HELP YOUR CHILDREN GET HOME SAFE

When you write a letter asking for something to be done for you, or for someone else, look for the basic factor most relevant to the person you are writing to. There are usually a number of factors and the trick is to choose the right ones for the other person.

The former American Secretary of State, Dr Henry Kissinger, appeared during his heyday to be able to work near miracles of persuasion. He was called the 'special negotiator' and seemed to have an exceptional gift for presenting the factors of a dispute so that each side saw the benefits to themselves of coming to an agreement.

This approach of adding value to words has never been put with more force than in the concept of the USP, a theory of advertising propounded by Rosser Reeves, who produced the television commercials for Eisenhower's presidential campaign.

If you haven't come across it, USP stands for Unique Selling Proposition. The theory is that every product or service has to offer something specific that nothing else can. And it has to be something people want. Here are some examples:

INTRODUCING THE ONLY SANDWICH BAG THAT REALLY KEEPS ITS MOUTH SHUT

Ziploc Sandwich Bags with a zipper-like seal that shuts the bag.

IF YOU'RE ROBBED ON HOLIDAY, THIS TRAVELLERS CHEQUE MAKES SURE YOUR HOLIDAY GOES ON

American Express travellers cheques offer a full refund usually on the same day you lose them.

THE LAST GAS STATION FOR 300 MILES

Sign outside a garage in the Australian Outback.

> Daddy's away abroad, so I'm the only one who can give you a cuppa in bed on Sunday.

A ten-year-old boy to his mother, making out a case for extra pocket money.

I'm the greatest!

Muhammad Ali.

The weakest kind of advertising is called 'me too' advertising. It says, 'You can buy this in a lot of other places but I also sell it.' Many sales letters say, in effect, 'We want you to buy what we are selling.' The inevitable reaction is, 'Thank you very much. But why should I ?'

Every time we want something done there has to be a reason why, or our letter, conversation or report end up as another 'me too' communication. It joins the queue with all the others unless we find something to make our case a special one.

There are times, of course, when there is nothing special that we can offer—except the way we offer it. David Ogilvy, the English advertising man in New York, was '. . . astonished to find how many manufacturers, even among the new generation, believe that women can be persuaded by logic and argument to buy one brand in preference to another, even if the brands are technically identical'.

When it is not what you say but the way you say it, you are involved in building an image. David Ogilvy did this for a little known shirt manufacturer. He put in every advertisement a man with a black eye-patch. This was 'The Man in the Hathaway Shirt', an image of confidence, virility and courage. It caught on, helped perhaps by Moshe Dayan, the heroic Israeli general, who wears a black eye-patch.

Ogilvy even ran full-page colour advertisements in the *New Yorker* without a single word, not even the name Hathaway. But everyone knew it was a Hathaway shirt in the ad—the man had a black eye-patch.

People have loyalty towards a brand of cigarettes, although tests show that they cannot tell their favourite brand from several others. Mary Wells Lawrence, the leading woman in American advertising, explains, 'You have to realise that when you buy a cigarette, part of what you buy is the image of yourself smoking that cigarette.'

Benson and Hedges cigarettes come in a gold-coloured box and gold is the theme of all the advertising. On posters and in colour ads, they can even leave out the brand name so long as there is enough gold around. In 1978 when the gold treasures of El Dorado were brought to England for a dazzling show at the Royal Academy, you can guess whose name was publicly linked with the exhibition.

We cannot help being in the image business. Our image is projected by the clothes we wear, the food we eat, the places we are seen in—and the words we use.

Try this test next time you get a letter from someone you don't know. Forget the facts it is telling you and ask what it tells you about the person who wrote it. Now take one of your own letters and try to read it as if you do not know who wrote it. Don't look at the arguments and requests you are making. Just ask what kind of a person would have written that letter. And is that image going to help your case?

Compare these extracts from two letters received by a finance company:

Letter 1

I understand that you are sometimes prepared to advance capital to people who want to expand their business.

My wife and I run two sandwich bars in this town, serving sandwiches and coffee for lunch to men and women who work in nearby offices. Our turnover has been going up each year for the last three years, and we have also started a send-out service of coffee in plastic mugs with lids.

We hope to open two more bars of the same kind in other parts of the town and we have been looking out for suitable premises.

Letter 2

My wife and I have spent two years working in Health Food Restaurants, because we want to make a go of one for ourselves.

We are young, in our early thirties, full of enthusiasm ourselves for eating fresh salads, wholemeal bread, free-range eggs, cheeses on the rind and other kinds of natural foods. That is the kind of food we are going to serve to our customers, who will be people working in offices.

We know from our experience and from asking around that more and more people are interested in eating natural foods, so the tide is going our way.

We are confident that we have found the perfect premises. There are a lot of office people working in the area, but there is no other Health Food Restaurant or salad bar anywhere near.

They are both good letters. But what would you think the writers are like? The finance company executive thought the first letter came from a rather quiet middle-aged couple, who were running a couple of ordinary sandwich bars. The couple who sent the second letter seemed to be young, go-ahead and full of good ideas and ambition.

He was wrong about the first couple. They are still in their twenties. Their two sandwich bars are attractive, with old stripped-pine counters and stools. They sell a variety of delicious sandwiches with inventive fillings such as shrimps with home-made mayonnaise and shredded lettuce; ham and pineapple; and cheese with grated nuts and dates. The second couple turned out to be much as he had expected. They are lively, with a lot of drive and energy.

It is not the information in those two letters that makes the difference. In fact, the writer of *Letter 1* had more to offer, because the business was already started and going well. The letters gave different impressions because of the images they projected of the people who had written them.

A run-of-the-mill expected way of putting down what you want to say usually produces a rather low-level response. One of the cleverest creative men in American advertising was asked to address an advertising convention. He called his talk 'How to be Different'. Sometimes it takes a lot of effort and head-breaking to find a different and effective way of saying something. But it is worth it because of all the added value your words take along with them.

Many makes of cars talk about good road-holding. The writer of the ads for the new Chevrolet *Camaro* worked hard at being different:

GO OUT AND HUG A ROAD YOU LIKE

Roads and Camaros.
When it comes to hugging, there hasn't been
anything like them since Romeo and Juliet.

He gives all the reasons: steel-belted radial tyres, a front stabiliser bar, low lines, power steering and a positive drive. At the end, he says pick the model you want and 'Then go out hug a road!'

Building societies all seem much the same: monumentally dull financial institutions. The old and respectable Woolwich Equitable Building Society decided to be different. They let their hair down in a series of fifteen-second spots on television, using stock comedy situations to put over the neatly alliterative slogan 'We're with the Woolwich!' One commercial showed a pantomime in rehearsal:

Producer   Are you Widder Twankey?
Panto dame   No, I'm widder Woolwich!

Another showed a group of Martians parking their flying saucer:

Traffic warden   Oi! Are you lot with that flying saucer?
Martians   No, we're with the Woolwich!

Building societies don't do that kind of thing, you might say. The Woolwich did and Donald Markham, their general manager, told me he hopes:

> Familiarity and good humour might suggest that such things as security and financial returns could go with the everyday, with shopping expeditions, with people of all types and ages.

Research is showing that more people are entrusting their money to the Woolwich Building Society because it is now well known to them. Being different has paid off.

When our words have added value they are worth more to us and to others. We have to start by having something to say. Then we must look for the value of what we say, not to ourselves, but to the other person. 'Do not', Bernard Shaw said, 'do unto others as you would they should do unto you. Their tastes may be different.'

7 How to come to a good end

Your last sentence is the last thing people read. It is your last chance to get through to them before signing your name. The last thing you say on the telephone before you hang up is the last thought you leave in the other person's mind. Your last words as you are leaving a meeting or an interview make the final impression for you. The way we end something can be even more important than the way we begin it, because people remember how things end.

Research on television commercials shows that the beginning and the end of a commercial are usually remembered best. The beginning because it is something new; and the end because that is what viewers see just before the next commercial comes up and takes their attention. It is the same with the end of your letter: that is the last thing someone takes in before going on to something else.

You cannot count on anyone reading anything a second time. At the best, people might skim through your letter again to remind themselves of what it is about. When that happens, they are more likely to read again in full your last sentence or paragraph. It is common to hope that the end of a letter or a report will tell us all we need to know about it.

If you watch people choosing a book in a library or book-shop, you will see them glancing through it, looking through the list of chapter headings, and then quite often turning to the last page. They want to see what comes at the end. Perhaps this is to avoid disappointment, because it's one thing to make a good beginning and something else to carry the same quality all the way through to the end.

When we say, 'All's well that ends well', we mean that even if things go wrong somewhere along the line, if it works out all right in the end, then we don't mind so much what has gone before. Our own experience confirms this. What at the time seems a disaster can be forgotten if something good comes out of it—in the end. A relationship can go through storms and tempests. If somehow it survives and there is understanding and harmony, the past sufferings seem unimportant. In show business, when everything is going wrong at the dress rehearsal, the cast and the desperate director are sustained by the determination and hope that it will be 'all right on the night'. That's all that matters.

In communication, getting off to a bad start is a setback, but coming to a bad end can mean total failure. When you are writing something or speaking to someone, you cannot always be sure to say just the right thing, no matter how hard you try. But if the last thing you say pulls it all together for you, your communication stands a good chance of success.

Many letters, meetings, telephone calls and love-affairs come to a bad end or just fizzle out. What happens is that we use all our energy writing or dictating an important letter, making a difficult telephone call or coping with an interview that a lot depends on. When it is nearly over, there is such a sense of relief that it's easy to be careless about what we say from then on. Or we fall back on some how's-your-father banality that means nothing and is a weak conclusion to our letter or conversation.

Most of us have experienced a let-down feeling after a telephone call, because we have allowed it to end in a feeble inconsequential way. We want to phone back to put it right but it is too late. The moment has gone. Even after a good meeting or interview, we can shut the conference room or office door behind us, with the uneasy thought that we have muffed the last minute or two. We have relaxed our concentration too soon instead of holding it to the last moment. In golf and tennis, and most other ball games, it is important, even *after* striking the ball, to follow-through, to carry the stroke all the way to the end.

81

It is human nature to sustain an almost superhuman effort as long as it seems necessary and then let go completely. Sprinters often flake out immediately they breast the tape, and oarsmen slump over their oars at the end of a boat race.

This happens in communication. It is quite a strain to write a letter that means a great deal to us, or to go through a meeting, an interview or even a telephone call that could affect our lives. So when it seems to be over, it is natural to feel relieved, although we still haven't written the last sentence, left the office or hung up the phone.

In communication, as in most other activities, following through all the way to the end is part of the action. When it is an important letter, treat the last sentence with a lot of respect. It is far too valuable to waste on anything like these examples:

I hope you will give this every consideration.

(From a man asking for a transfer from the north of England to the London office.)

Looking forward to hearing from you at your convenience.

(From the director of a company offering a demonstration of a new type of photo-copying machine.)

I am looking forward to receiving your application.

(From the head of one of the biggest charge-card services in the world.)

Do send me your subscription form today.

(From the circulation director of a leading US business magazine.)

Once again, please forgive me for not turning up for the appointment.

(From a girl who didn't arrive for an interview for a job.)

Although those were important letters to the people who wrote them, the endings are trite. They might just as well have been left out altogether because they add nothing of value. That is a waste because the last sentence of a letter can be decisive. At the least, it can make a contact with the reader. In some cases, it can make the difference between the whole thing being put on one side or something being done about it then and there.

Last words are important. Actresses and actors love a good exit line, because they leave the stage, not with a whimper, but with a bang that makes an impact for them on the audience. One of the great exit lines in literature is in Dickens' *Tale of Two Cities*. Sydney Carton, the wastrel of an English barrister, says this, as he saves another man's life by taking his place on the scaffold:

> It is a far, far better thing that I do than I have ever done; it is a far, far better rest that I go to, than I have ever known.

We are left feeling that he has, in the end, made up for everything that has gone before.

The most famous exit line in the history of films was Mae West's in *She Done Him Wrong*. She filled a doorway like the stuffing in a vol-au-vent, wiggled everything from fingertips to toe-nails and invited us to:

> Come up 'n' see me some time!

There is an easy way to give any important communication a good exit line. You do it by asking the following question: What do I want to happen next? What do you want to happen after whoever it is finishes reading your letter, after you hang up the phone or leave an office after a meeting? Sometimes it is worth writing down beforehand the answer to that question so that you are clear about it. Then all you have to do is embody that answer in your last sentence.

Advertisers know all about this. Delegates at international advertising film festivals, held each year in Cannes or Venice, come away after a week of looking at commercials from all over the world, knowing how to say in a whole lot of languages, 'Buy some tomorrow!'

That pay-off comes up at the end of TV commercials from every country. It is what the advertising business is about.

However calm and distinguished some advertisers pretend to be, that's what they want to happen, that's what they pay for. An American radio commercial, announcing a special offer for one week, ended:

Run! (Do not walk!) to your nearest drugstore and ask for . . .!

Perhaps that sounds a bit brash to English ears but to American housewives it conveyed the sense of urgency the advertiser wanted.

The most effective endings are action endings. You have someone's attention for a few minutes. Whoever it is has stopped whatever he was doing to read your letter or listen to you. Very soon the person who can help you will be interested in something else and for the time being will forget about you. If it is at all possible or appropriate, use your last sentence to ask them to do something. Make it as specific as you can and as short as you can.

Once again Winston Churchill gives a marvellous demonstration of how to do it. He is replying to President Roosevelt. 'We shall not fail or falter,' he says, 'We shall not weaken or tire . . .' Then comes his last sentence, short, definite and asking for action—'Give us the tools, and we will finish the job.'

It is well known in advertising practice that a coupon at the end of an advertisement multiplies the returns not just by two or three but by ten times and more. It gives readers something definite to do, instead of leaving them to think about something they might do later on. We have all seen advertisements and thought 'I must do something about that'. The moment passes and we forget.

A former Canadian Mounted Policeman got a job in advertising by sending up a note by hand to the head of Lord and Thomas, which was then the most successful advertising agency in the United States. His last sentence read:

If you wish to know what advertising is, send the word YES down by the messenger.

84

The request for immediate action worked. The boss came down himself and over a drink in a nearby bar heard the oracle. In case you are interested, he was told that advertising is 'Salesmanship in print', which still holds up as a good definition.

Here are some other examples of endings that led to immediate and specific action. A mother wrote to the headmaster of her daughter's school. Sally, her daughter, who was fourteen, showed exceptional musical talent and her mother wanted her to have extra piano lessons in place of other subjects. She ended her letter:

> I know it is not easy to rearrange time-tables for individual pupils, so I would not ask it unless I felt it is really important to Sally. If you can do this for her, we should all be very grateful. If you want to discuss it, please telephone me. I shall stay in all this morning, waiting.

The managing director of a medium-sized manufacturing company received a complaint from an important customer. His reply ended:

> You are a special customer, so I want to put the matter right and see that it never happens again. Would you let me send over a working party of three to meet their opposite numbers working for you, so that we can see how to stop anything going wrong in future?
>
> Here is a list of dates and times when our people are able, ready and very willing to come along. Please tick the most convenient time and send it back to me personally.

A girl sent a good promotion idea to the managing director of a store. Her letter ended:

> Somebody is going to cash-in on this idea. Before anyone else does, can I tell you more about it? I'll telephone your secretary Wednesday morning, 7th May. If it's all right with you, please give her a time when I can come to see you.

This is the ending of a letter from a wine merchant selling off, after Christmas, what are known in the trade as 'bin-ends':

These left-overs are marked well down in price. We have a lot of customers, so the best we can do is to make it 'first come first served'.

This is a real chance to buy better wines at the same price as you've been paying for something much more ordinary. We'd love to think of you drinking them. But help us not to disappoint you, by going through the list now. And please send your order today—and be one of the lucky ones.

Those are four different situations. But the endings all do one thing: they ask for action and make it clear what that action is. Three of the endings do even better. They give a time-limit. Always look for the possibility of giving a time-limit, when you can do that without arousing resentment in the other person, because a time-limit is the most effective way of getting action. A distinguished newspaper editor used to say to young reporters who were late with their copy 'I don't want it good. I don't want it bad. I want it in half an hour.'

Here is a useful test of the effectiveness of any last sentence. Cover it up. If it makes no real difference to the letter, you have come to a bad end. Try this on the four letters quoted above. Cover the last sentence and you will see there is a loss of energy, drive and purpose. If that happens when you cover one of your last sentences, you have a good ending and can send off your letter with a good heart.

When you are making an important telephone call, you have the advantage of being able to plan it. You can write down what you are going to say first. And you can write down what you are going to say at the end. Then it is there in front of you, even if you have to change it round a little to meet the circumstances.

You can plan your last words at an interview, so that you go out saying something that will help your case. When you have said it, the best thing is to finish and say no more. A feeling of insecurity often makes us go on beyond the point of real usefulness. That can easily make an encounter end on a weak note instead of a positive one.

At that macabre banquet in Macbeth's palace, when Banquo's ghost turns up as an uninvited and unwelcome guest,

86

the other visitors are slow to leave. Lady Macbeth tells them not to hang about:

> Stand not upon the order of your going,
> But go at once.

At a meeting or an interview, if you have come up with a good exit line, the next thing to do is to exit.

Here is a collection of good ways that people have ended meetings and interviews. We start with a chairman at the end of an annual general meeting:

> Before I sit down, can I tell you this? We think of the shareholders as our friends, because without you there would be no business. Sometime at nearly every board meeting, I ask this question: 'Will it be good for the shareholders?'

A headmistress ended her address to parents:

> We see ourselves as working with you to help your sons and daughters. Will you think of yourselves as working with us? When there are disagreements and irritations, please remember this— we are both on the *same* side.

A representative from the shop-floor ended his case to the works manager for a new procedure to increase production and hence productivity bonuses:

> Give us a chance to try this out for two weeks. If there are any headaches to begin with, I'll work late to put them right and give my overtime pay to any charity you name.

A girl at the end of an interview for a job:

> I've got enthusiasm and I want to do well. That can't be bad, can it?

We learn something important from readership tests of advertisements. They show what happens when people read our letters and memos. Their interest is at a higher level to begin with because they are reading something new; and as we have seen, our first sentence can make that interest much higher still. They read the body of the letter to see what it says and then towards the end, attention and interest tend to fall off.

Observe yourself when you are reading letters and you will often see the flow of your interest following the same downward curve towards the end. Suppose it is a letter giving an estimate for building work. You want to see right away how much it is. From then on, your interest and attention drop away and you just glance at the last sentence. Research and recall tests of advertisements regularly show this pattern.

We are more successful at getting through to someone when we are sensitive to how they are likely to respond at each stage. If we change the usual response by lifting their attention at the end of an important letter, we leave them more receptive towards us.

We know that a request for action right at the end of a letter gets the adrenalin flowing. Another good ending is to ask a question. It works in headlines and it also works in last sentences.

This is a question at the end of a letter from a bank manager introducing customers to a new automated cashier system:

> We look after your money twenty-four hours a day, so don't you think it is fair you should be able to use it twenty-four hours a day?

A secretarial agency wrote to local firms and also used a question to end their letter:

> Do you want temporary secretaries and typists who are good value because they are thoroughly tested *before* they are sent to you?

A letter from a parliamentary candidate to his constituents finished up:

> After all, do you want a member who believes he is in Parliament to look after your interests—more than anything else?

Asking a question at the end of a letter is like keeping up your voice at the end of a sentence—it keeps people interested and with you.

People at the top everywhere are under a lot of strain and the pressure is always on them to turn to the next thing. They are making decisions all day long and it is a relief for them not to have to think something through right away. At the end of a communication, try if you can to make a positive suggestion about what the next step could be, even if it's no more than 'Please let me know a time when I can come to talk about this'. That would take you further along in the direction you want to go.

In our lives we do not write only business letters. We write to people we love and to our friends. Sometimes these letters have to traverse the world and take with them comfort, good humour and greetings. When we are writing to someone we care about, the ending of our letter is just as important—it can carry our feelings along with it.

In New York I was visiting a girl in hospital and she showed me a letter from her mother in England. This was the last sentence:

> When you are feeling low, remember this my dear—I am with you all the time.

Sydney Smith, a lovable and good-natured clergyman, gave this advice at the end of a short note to Lucy, who was on her way to Boulogne:

> Don't marry anybody who has not a tolerable understanding and a thousand a year, and God bless you, dear child!

In 1835, when that letter was written, a thousand pounds a year could set you up in luxury and comfort.

This is the last sentence of a much sadder letter. The courage and feeling of the man who wrote it still come through. In the best tradition of good communication, Robert Falcon Scott, near to the South Pole, uses his last sentence for the most important request he has left:

> These rough notes and our dead bodies must tell the tale, but surely, surely, a great rich country like ours will see that those who are dependent on us are properly provided for.

Next, the ending of a letter full of good humour and friendliness. Charles MacArthur and Ben Hecht were journalists in Chicago, who worked together and wrote comedies together.

89

MacArthur had taken James, his sixteen-year-old son, on holiday to Venezuela. His letter back to his old friend, Ben Hecht, ends up:

> Jim won the ship's ping-pong contest. He doesn't want to be called Jamie any more, and is chasing a blonde my size. Time sure flies.
> Sunburned salutes to you all.

Ending telephone calls is difficult. We all know how easy it is to let them ramble on until the whole point and all the feeling are lost. Or we end them abruptly so the other person feels cut off. The only way to do better is to be alert and decide in advance how you want to leave the person you are speaking to. Someone I love once said this to me at the end of a long-distance call and I still remember it warmly:

> That was a marvellous conversation. It was just like having you here in the room beside me.

I heard another telephone call end like this. It was a man talking to his wife, whose father had just died:

> If I were with you, darling, I'd put my arms around you and hold you very close. Imagine that's just what I'm doing right now.

The telephone can be as cold and sterile as a surgeon's scalpel or it can be as warm as a red rose. It all depends upon what we say and how we say it.

We have to work hard to arrive at a good ending to any communication. We have to think of what we want that valuable last sentence or paragraph to do for us or for someone else. And we have to find the words in time. The rewards make it all worthwhile. If we get it right, our communication stands a good chance of bringing about what we want to happen next. Or it brings warmth or comfort into someone's life.

Almost anything is better than letting a letter, a meeting or a telephone call drag on. 'Begin at the beginning,' the King said gravely in *Alice in Wonderland*, 'and go on till you come to the end. Then stop.'

I've got the message.

8 Psycho-linguistics

How to pick good words
and avoid bad ones

Dictionaries deal with the meaning of words. But that is only part of the picture because words contain something else. Dr Carl Gustav Jung, the great psychologist and healer, discovered that words are also full of symbols. By a symbol, he meant something that triggers off a response deep within us so that we react, often without knowing why. For Jung:

> . . . a word or an image is symbolic when it implies something more than its obvious and immediate meaning. It has a wider 'unconscious' aspect that is never precisely defined or fully explained.

Psycho-linguistics is the study of the interrelation between words and our minds and emotions. It is taught hardly anywhere and you will not find it in many dictionaries, although it is included in the new *Concise Oxford Dictionary* 1976 edition. We have to know something about it if we want our words to get through for us in the right way.

All the time we are reading or listening, writing or speaking, we are involved in psycho-linguistics because we are being affected, and are affecting others, not only by what the words are saying but by their emotional charge and the underlying meanings people associate with them.

Many words are like stones with three facets. The first facet is the straightforward meaning you find in the dictionary. The second is something symbolic that affects us in a rather vague way that we do not fully understand. The third is another meaning that has been built up by images we have come to associate with a particular word. When this last meaning becomes strong enough, it takes over as the regular dictionary meaning. But long before that happens, this other meaning affects us whenever we read or hear the word.

Not so long ago it was all right, in this country, to call someone a capitalist. 1959 Oxford dictionaries say that a capitalist is a person who uses capital in business; a lot of people do that. But now Karl Marx has won and people object to being called capitalists because they would feel accused of exploiting the people who work for them. The associated meaning of capitalist has taken over and capitalists prefer to be called industrialists.

Most of us are very happy to drink champagne, when we get the chance, but would not like to be accused of drinking 'intoxicating liquor'. That is a perfectly accurate description of champagne but, thanks to psycho-linguistics, it turns a pleasure into a vice.

A nudist, even in the latest dictionaries, is someone who goes around naked because it is healthy. But no one wants to be called a nudist any more because the word connects up with exhibitionism and strip-tease shows. A BBC reporter said 'nude' rhymes with lewd, rude and crude. If you enjoy walking around naked, the in-word is naturists which has a nice comfortable feeling of living naturally and simply. No one cares if it makes all the rest of us unnaturists. With words it's every man for himself.

One day, a year or so back, the *Daily Telegraph* ran this headline on the front page:

CALLAGHAN 'TOO BUSY' TO HEAR COGGAN'S
. APPEAL

Almost every word is loaded with associated meanings. The unprefixed surnames diminish the stature of both men. When we say we are too busy, we usually mean we can't be bothered. And the headline writer made it worse by adding quotation marks—'too busy'. The word 'appeal' carries with it the suggestion of a request for help or mercy. We are left feeling that the Prime Minister couldn't be bothered to take time off to listen to a humanitarian request from the Archbishop.

The associated meanings disappear when the headline is rewritten:

MR CALLAGHAN UNABLE TO MEET ARCHBISHOP

As the Goons used to say, it's all in the mind, which is what psycho-linguistics is about.

This headline was unflattering to Michael Foot:

FOOT HANGS ON TO LEADERSHIP

It makes us think of someone hanging on to a cliff by his fingertips. The unprefixed surname makes Mr Foot seem even more desperate. See what a different feeling this gives:

MICHAEL FOOT RETAINS LEADERSHIP

The Christian name and surname together are friendly. The word 'retains' gives a feeling of confidence and ability.

Even on the telephone maybe we should think twice before saying 'hang on', because it leaves someone out on a limb. 'I'll be back with you in a moment' is more encouraging. Perhaps it doesn't matter much on the phone, but it's worth being aware of the difference.

At the end of a letter quoted earlier, a girl wrote, 'Please forgive me for not turning up for the appointment.' If you have ever been left waiting under a clock tower or in the foyer of a hotel, 'not turning up' echoes resentful memories. If she wrote 'Please forgive me for being unable to keep our appointment,' the other person might feel less negative about it.

Some words can affect our mood, our state of mind and even our physical state. When we are talking to someone, we are often aware we have said something that has upset them: there is a reaction or change of mood. This gives us a chance to put things right. But when we use the wrong words in a letter, we are not there to see the effect. I once saw an intelligent publisher hopping mad, waving about a letter and shouting 'What the hell does he mean writing to me like this?'

The letter was asking a favour and I was sure the writer had no idea it would get that reaction. He had used unintentionally, or at least without conscious intent, words with a powerful negative symbolism. Psycho-linguistics was at work. It is easy to see what a mess it can make of things when we are using words to help someone or to ask someone to help us.

The following experiment has demonstrated how much

words affect us. If you saw it carried out, as I have, you would always be on guard against certain words. The word HOPE-LESS is printed in large letters on a card or projected on to a screen and someone is asked to look at it for several minutes. The images associated with that word begin to take over and you see the person's face change. With some people, their pulse-rate drops.

Other words like PATIENCE and COURAGE will develop a positive attitude. Word-therapy of this kind is used in some clinics and hospital wards. The large display of the word SILENCE in some libraries not only makes people speak in hushed voices, it can make them feel quiet and reflective.

This has been compared to colours in a room. In a room facing north, designers use pinks, reds and browns because they are 'warm' colours. Certain colours can make us feel low-spirited; others make us light-hearted. Tests have been carried out using two reception rooms with different colour schemes, letting visitors choose which room they wait in. The results show that people are strongly attracted to certain colours and put off by others. Like words, colours work on us as symbols and connect with feelings and experiences beyond our conscious recall.

Advertising agencies are aware that they have to find out how people react to words, pictures, colours and ideas. It is not enough just to ask them, because people will often respond to things in ways they themselves do not know about or understand.

When a new brand of sherry was being launched, regular sherry drinkers were shown three different labels. They put them in order of preference. The advertising agency was doubtful about the result and was advised by a psychologist to carry out a different test.

This time the same sherry was put into three bottles with the different labels on them. People tasted a glass from each bottle and listed the sherries in order of quality. Hardly anyone said all three sherries were the same: there were marked preferences.

When these were averaged out the result was not the same as the straight label test.

People may prefer certain colours and designs of labels but they associate other colours and designs with good sherry. If you are selling sherry, that's what counts. A brilliant designer might produce a beautiful label but if the associations are wrong, it would not sell sherry.

In another test, women were given a pat of butter and a pat of margarine to compare. The margarine was yellow and the butter was white. More than ninety per cent of the women picked out the yellow pat as butter. Perhaps because it is the colour of sunshine and buttercups, people associate yellow with freshly churned butter. The association is so strong that it has a stronger influence even than the taste.

At one time margarine manufacturers worked hard and unsuccessfully to make us pronounce 'margarine' with a hard 'g', as in 'bargain'; they wanted to break away from the negative association of 'marge'.

In the early days of instant coffee, advertisers got off to a bad start by stressing words such as 'quick', 'time-saving', 'efficient'. These are all words without warmth and feeling. Makers of fresh coffee fought back with warm happy words—'aroma', 'flavour', 'rich', 'fresh'. Makers of instant coffee soon learned the lesson and changed to the warmest, most appetising words they could find.

It is futile to fight strong associations that exist in people's minds. Certain words and ideas make us react in a particular way, leave us more helpful or less helpful, move us towards something or pull us away from it. When we want to get through to people, we can use these forces to work for us.

Here is another way to understand this vital aspect of language. Next time you get a letter that affects your emotions to an extent that seems out of proportion to what has been said, spend a few minutes looking closely at the words. You might find out what has caused your mood and made you depressed, irritable or pleased with life.

Dr Jung believed that many of these feelings are part of the inheritance of the human condition, just as the human body has a long evolutionary history behind it. He called them *archetypes* and compared them to the impulse of birds to build nests, or ants to form organised colonies. Most of us know from our dreams that our unconscious is teeming with ideas and connections that can upset or disturb us at any moment, just as there are other associations that make us feel secure and comfortable. When on a bleak cold day, we sit by a crackling log fire, it is not only the warmth that draws us, but a deeply felt response to a symbol of security.

All this may seem remote stuff when you are sitting down to write a letter, dictating to your secretary or picking up the telephone. But everyone who uses words successfully to sell, convince, inspire or comfort must develop an awareness of the feeling behind the meaning of words.

We need to be particularly careful when we are making or dealing with a complaint, because that is a situation where we can in a flash spark off resentment, fear or aggression. From then on, it is an uphill job to get something put right. We need not be conciliatory but it is wise to look at our words extra carefully. Otherwise we trigger off a negative reaction that affects the way someone acts on our letter. Read these two letters written to a department store, complaining about a faulty electric toaster:

Letter 1
I am writing to complain about the electric toaster I bought from you only last week.
No matter what I do with the regulator switch, the toast is always burnt.

The moment anyone reads 'I am writing to complain', the reaction is 'here comes trouble' and up come defences and resistance. If you want to, you can take it all the way back to childhood, when we were afraid of being scolded or smacked for doing something wrong. If you think that is fanciful, check your own reaction next time someone picks on you.

Letter 2

I thought how much you would like to know that the assistant who served me in your electrical department last week couldn't have been more helpful.

In spite of that though, there is something not right with the regulator on the toaster that I bought, because the toast keeps coming out burnt.

The woman who wrote that worked at avoiding negative reactions. She even wrote 'not right' instead of 'wrong'. The first letter produced a reply asking for the toaster to be brought in for repair. The second letter resulted in someone telephoning to say a new toaster was being sent and the other one would be collected at the same time.

Words change the way we feel about things. An unofficial strike or lock-out sounds irresponsible and aggressive. For a while, everyone felt better when it was called 'industrial action'; that sounded more positive and disciplined. But by now the words 'industrial action' have become dirty words. Even good words turn sour if they are used too often in a bad sense.

When the Writers' Guild of Great Britain recently advertised a charitable holiday retreat for writers, they wrote 'By the terms of the trust non-men are excluded'. In trying to avoid problems by excluding non-men, rather than women, they walked into a much worse trap: non-men has a strong flavour of inadequacy like non-event and non-starter. Words get us into trouble if we are not alert to their associations.

On a BBC programme, Len Murray of the TUC said 'negotiations with the government are at an end'. For Denis Healey, a government minister, it was 'a pause to let the dust settle'. They were both talking about the same breakdown in discussions.

No one knows how much disruption in our society, at all levels, is caused by the wrong words being used. Sometimes we can hear it going on. In a BBC news broadcast, industrial action by ASLEF, the train drivers' union, was described by a representative of British Rail as 'stupid unofficial action'. The editor of the *Sunday Times,* which had ceased publication because of a dispute with a union, called the union's attitude 'idiot logic'. Perhaps both statements were justified. What is sure is that words like 'stupid' and 'idiot' arouse strong negative emotions and keep both sides away from the conference table.

It is worth looking very hard at some of the words we are in the habit of using, in case we have forgotten what they sound like to other people. Because all of us relate to words. Some words make us feel good, other words make us feel bad. Publishers sell off cheaply unsold copies of books and call them publishers' remainders. But 'remainders' has an association of unappetising left-overs. Why not publishers' offers, which sounds generous and friendly? It is depressing to be an old age pensioner but you can hold your head up when you are called a senior citizen. It's charity when you apply for public assistance but social security is a right. And nobody wants the dole when they can get unemployment benefit.

The same things said in different ways can make people feel much better about them. Other times when descriptions are updated, something is lost. The Postmaster General sounds an approachable father-figure. The Chairman and Chief Executive of the Post Office Board (as he now is) seems distant and remote. Luckily the attempt to call postmen 'delivery officers' was thrown out by Parliament.

In a laboratory or Court of Law, precise definitions are essential. With people, it is more important for words to make them feel right. If the Chancellor of the Exchequer ever becomes the Chief Accountant it would, in our hearts, clip something off the value of the pound.

Even simple price tags can be manipulated to get a better reaction. Those old drapery shopkeepers who put 2/11¾d on a price ticket knew what they were doing. It kept the price on the right side of the three shilling barrier. The price ticket game still goes on but these days the stakes are much higher. Recently a new pocket television set was advertised 'for just £99.95', which keeps it on the right side of the hundred pound barrier.

Our reactions to these things are not logical. They are none-theless real and affect our attitudes. If you have to keep some-one waiting, perhaps it is better to say 'It will be ready in fifty-five minutes' instead of 'It will be ready in an hour'. We feel better if we have a month's holiday rather than four weeks; and would rather have a special price than a cut price. Humans are a compound of irrational feelings and logical intellect but our experience of ourselves and our relationships with others show it is feelings that carry the day more often.

Games with words have a way of making us respond. Psychologists shy away from any attempt to explain and analyse that indefinable, indispensable and apparently exclusively human attribute—a sense of humour. All we know is that when it is activated we feel good.

Word-play is often a form of punning and puns are usually derided. Yet Shakespeare enjoyed fooling around with words. When it is well done, word-play can still make us give friendly and sympathetic attention to something. Here are some nice examples:

GREEN SHIELD FORECASTS LESS STICKY TIMES

(The title of an article about how Green Shield stamps were trying to make a recovery with new incentive and promotion schemes.)

SCOTCH ON THE ROCKS

(The title of a piece by a city editor about the financial prob-lems of the Scotch whisky industry.)

Affordable Norway

(From the Norwegian National Tourist Office about low price holidays in Norway.)

Stuff the bird! What about the Pudding?

(Advertising a Christmas pudding.)

Winston Churchill played games with the *sound* of words. If you listen to recordings of war-time speeches, you will hear him pronounce Nazis as *Nahzies*, so they sound like the 'nasties' in a children's fairy story, unpleasant, distasteful and to be overcome.

There are warm words and cold words, as there are warm and cold colours. Warm words make us feel secure and comfortable. Cold words leave us uneasy, give us doubts or put us completely against something. Cold words have their place but only when the situation calls for them.

We get a new feeling about words when we look at them in this way. Here are some examples of warm and cold words to show how you can use psycho-linguistics to get through to people in the best way possible.

A few warm words:

Agree When someone says 'I completely agree with you' we get a warm glow. When something is agreeable, it is pleasant. We like being agreeably surprised.

Basic Something that is basic feels firm, solid and reliable. A basic proposition or a basic idea suggests that it is founded on sensible first principles.

Broad-based A stage further than 'basic'. Something broad-based is not going to topple easily. It is not just a flash in the pan but sound and secure.

Care A very comforting word. It is reassuring to be told 'We care very much about doing our best for you'. The phrase 'couldn't care less' is chilling.

Fair Full of good associations. There is 'the fair sex', 'My Fair Lady', 'None but the brave deserve the fair'. If something is 'fair enough', we don't argue about it. Phrases such as 'It seems fair to suggest', 'fair to ask' help to disarm argument.

If we have to back down over something and write or say 'It seems fair to agree', we turn a negative into a positive.

Forward-looking It is human nature to be apprehensive about what might happen next. When we hear the words forward-looking we feel more secure, because someone has looked at least as far as the end of the road, even if not around the corner.

Good The word has the same origin as God and our warm response to it is archetypal. Use it when you can.

Gratitude One of the warmest feelings one human being can have towards another. A good word to use.

Heart The heart is the pulse of life. It is a word that can move us when we read it or hear it used: 'with all my heart', 'heart-felt', 'Your letter gives me much heart.'

Hope An old Anglo-Saxon word. It is almost impossible to keep going without hope. Dante chose the right words for the doors of hell—'All hope abandon, ye who enter here'.

When there is nothing else you can say in a situation at least use the word 'hope'. It keeps the door open.

Independent It carries with it a warm feeling of being un-biased, open-minded, objective, free. It was good psycho-linguistics to call the alternative television service 'independent television' instead of 'commercial television'. (See 'commercial' in the list of cold words.)

Love A marvellous word to use when you can. Even when things are as drab as can be, it is a word that can make life still worth living. Perhaps it is the warmest word in English.

New Paradoxically one of the very old words in English, going back beyond Anglo-Saxon to Old Norse. Although it has been used so much in advertising, research continues to show that 'new' still has a lot of life left in it. Dr Ernest Dichter, the motivational research psychologist, urged copywriters to use 'new' in their headlines whenever possible.

Simplicity John Tessimond, the poet who was an advertising copywriter, wrote:

One day people will touch and talk perhaps easily,
And loving be natural as breathing and warm as sunlight,
And people will untie themselves, as string is unknotted,
Unfold and yawn and stretch and spread their fingers,
Unfurl, uncurl like seaweed returned to the sea,
And work will be simple and swift as a seagull flying,
And play will be casual and quiet as a seagull settling,
And the clocks will stop, and no one will wonder or care or notice,
And people will smile without reason, even in the winter, even in the rain.

Most of us yearn for a life free from complications. That's why simplicity is such a very warm word.

Sincere A reader just glosses over 'Yours sincerely' at the end of a letter. But a sentence that begins 'I sincerely believe . . .' makes us read it in a different way.

Special Everyone feels someone special. So we all like the idea of getting special attention, special consideration or a special offer. Use this word when you want to make someone interested.

Young It goes back to Anglo-Saxon so it has been in the language a long time. But it is still lively, with echoes of spring, freshness and enthusiasm.

Cold words are words in the shadow. Politicians often use them about opposition parties. We have to use words like these sometimes but should always be aware of the effect they have on people. Here are a few:

Abnormal A sinister word that makes people uneasy.

Afraid A word that goes with darkness and gloom. It is often used unnecessarily:

> I'm afraid it will be another five minutes.
> We are afraid that we cannot accept your order without payment in advance.
> I'm afraid he can't see you at the moment.

Of course this is just a manner of speaking. But why link up with a negative emotion when it can be avoided?

> Just five minutes and it will be all ready.
> We look forward to dealing with your order, although please send payment in advance.
> I'm sorry he's engaged at the moment.

But This little word is double-edged. It can put people on guard or can encourage them. If you say 'It's very good but . . .', your 'but' will produce an immediate reaction of caution. If you say, 'It will be very difficult but . . .', your 'but' gives hope. It is a word to watch. Be especially careful of 'Yes, but . . .' 'Although' is a useful word to substitute.

Cannot Look at these sentences from actual letters:

> We cannot deliver in three weeks.
> I cannot get it done for you.

'Cannot' is a rejecting word that leaves the other person out in the cold. You can get a better reaction sometimes by avoiding it:

Can you give us five weeks for delivery?
I'm sorry it's not possible to do it.

Cash in It has a strong flavour of opportunism. Be careful about telling someone they are cashing in on a situation, unless you mean to attack them. On the other hand, it's all right to 'make the most' of anything. Same man—different hat.

Commercial Of course this word has a perfectly harmless and legitimate use, but sometimes carries with it the suggestion of being more interested in profits than quality and integrity— 'the commercial theatre', 'too commercial'. It is a word to watch.

Disappoint When we write or say, 'I'm sorry to disappoint you . . .', we are inviting people to feel more disappointed than they might have been.

Disagree Look at the other person's face when you say, 'I disagree with you.' There will nearly always be a defensive reaction. This happens very often at meetings and a lot of time and energy are wasted. I have heard these other ways used to side-step a conflict:

Can we look at it another way?
Would you consider another point of view?
Here's something else worth looking at.

Dislike Another rejecting word that should be used only if you do not want to be warmer and more friendly.

Doubt Most people have doubts about many things. Why remind them and make them hesitate? You could change 'Although you may have some doubts' to 'Although you may want to consider this'.

Risk The word often makes people react irrationally. Lord Rothschild, in a lecture he called *Risk*, said there is no such thing as a risk-free society. He quoted an old Chinese proverb to show that even a simple life has risk: 'The couple who go to bed early to save candles end up with twins'.

What matters is the degree of risk. Is it one in a million or one in ten? When people read or hear the word 'risk', they often don't ask that question, so we risk putting them off.

Unfair and Unreasonable Both are words of accusation and nearly always produce a strong defensive attitude in return. Be careful about using them, unless you want a fight.

Unfortunately A depressing word used many times un-necessarily:

Unfortunately we weren't able to get in touch with you.
Unfortunately we cannot accept it.
Unfortunately the price is too high.

As a result, a negative statement becomes even more nega-tive.

There are thousands more warm and cold words. When you get into the habit of looking at the emotional colouring of words, as well as their meanings, you will find yourself using more good words and avoiding as many of the bad ones as you can.

9 Face to face

The same things make our communications successful whether we are writing to a company on the other side of the world, shouting to a man on the other side of the road or speaking to a woman three feet away. We always have to get their attention, keep their interest and relate to them as one human being to another.

But when we send a letter, words are everything. Take them away and all that is left is a blank sheet of paper or just a letter-heading. When we are speaking to someone face to face, words are only part of the communication between us. Take them away and all kinds of messages still pass across.

Peter Brook, the theatre producer, uses experiments in communication without words. He asks actors to express feelings and thoughts by using their eyes or the back of the head or just by movement of the torso, keeping the arms and legs still. In an actors' studio in New York, I saw a girl express what she was feeling by nothing more than coming into the room and sitting down. Although nothing was said, a remarkably clear message came through.

Dr David Mendel, a consultant at St Thomas's Hospital, London, believes doctors should learn to read patients' faces to help with diagnosis. He says that even when a patient is silent:

> His face is talking and may sometimes be wildly signalling . . . When he listens to the doctor, the reception of each word is registered on his face and if the doctor ignores this running commentary on his 'spiel', he is a fool.

If you turn off the sound on a television set, you still understand a lot of what is going on. Sydney Newman, the Canadian

105

producer who did so much to develop television drama, tells us:

> I well remember getting fed to the teeth telling good radio and
> stage writers that to learn how to write for the camera, they should
> imagine that all their characters are ninety per cent mute.

Until it is demonstrated to them, most people think that
when they are face to face with someone, they have to use words
in the same way as when writing letters or reports. At interviews and meetings, if you expect words to do the whole job
of communication, you will probably use too many words.
And that dilutes their effect.

Sitting opposite someone, you need less words because
your face and body help to convey your meaning and so does
the way you speak. The other person unconsciously expects
this because he is looking and listening instead of reading. If you
sit without movement or expression and talk in a flat voice,
communication is at half cock.

There is no need, of course, to wave our arms about and give
a performance. That would be distracting. But it is important
to be aware how we can help our words work harder when we
are talking directly to someone. Small things can have a big
effect.

Leaning forward in your chair can underline the sincerity of
what you are saying. Looking away and then looking back at
the other person can make words seem more considered. A
smile can turn a simple 'thank you' into an expression of deep
gratitude. Putting a hand on someone's shoulder and looking
into their eyes can say all the words in our heart at that moment.

These are only examples because what is natural for one
person does not work for another. All of us have to find our
own gestures and expressions. A woman uses different ones
from a man. What is effective for a man of fifty can be all
wrong for someone of twenty-five and, more important still,
the other way round.

Our age, our style and the situation all affect the ways we
can help our words to get through successfully at meetings and

interviews. Some people find they communicate much more effectively just by saying less. These things are personal and individual and cannot be forced. But as we become more aware of the possibilities, our own style develops naturally.

When we are talking to someone, their attention is not focused in the same way as when they are reading a letter. An encounter between two people is always a little strange and mysterious because there are so many psychic reactions: shyness, fears, anxieties, memories, dreams, longings, fill the space between us and another person.

If it is someone we know, all the circumstances of our relationship are touched. Status often gets in the way—too often— and then nobody thinks straight or talks straight because they are too conscious of their own position or of someone else's. With a stranger, there are all the associations of type, looks, age, personality and sex.

We may appear to have a captive audience because someone is there listening. But their thoughts are not captive. They could be all over the place. So shorter sentences, simpler words and straightforward expressions stand a much better chance of getting through successfully.

Speaking slowly encourages someone to take us seriously. Speaking too fast usually transmits uncertainty to the other person. Margaret Thatcher tells us, '. . . when you're terribly nervous, your voice does tend to rise—and the cure is to try to be more relaxed . . . You're frightened to death—but never mind!' A young actress passed on this advice to me: 'As I feel my heart beating faster, I concentrate on talking slowly and my nervousness goes or at least doesn't run away with me.'

There is no point in shouting: it is always more difficult to understand words when they are being said too loud. A successful chief executive in America has the habit of saying in the midst of a heated meeting, 'Not so loud please. I can't hear you.'

The most common fault in face-to-face communication is saying too much too quickly. You can re-read a letter if you don't understand something. But you cannot re-read an interview. If a letter is too long, you can pick out the points that matter: if someone talks too much, the wood disappears among the trees.

We can draft and re-draft an important letter as often as we like. But a meeting or interview is a one-night stand and we cannot write the whole script in advance. How do we find the words we need when there's no time to think about them?

The best advice is to go back to the basic principle of all good communication. Make sure you know precisely what result you want and keep your attention on that. Then the words you say will lead in the direction you want to go which is much more important than saying something clever.

When we convince people, reassure them or comfort them, we do not use clever words. Clever words are for parliamentary arguments, debating societies and TV quiz shows. In most other situations there is a natural suspicion of over persuasiveness. Oversell puts people off: you see them walking away in the market-place when a salesman puts on too much pressure.

With someone we care about, simplicity is all. After a long talk with her father, a daughter wrote:

'Talk is cheap' they say, and some talk is undoubtedly cheap— but one is alone in the end with one's problems and unhappiness, and the words of another can be just enough to keep one going on and trying once again—that is what your words bring me.

Not clever words, but only a simple expression of our common humanity can do what that girl described.

The president of one of the great Oxford colleges is a surprisingly quiet and gentle man, who nevertheless has to control meetings of the governing body. He gave me this as his secret:

When it is something very important, I try not to sound too serious about it, because that makes everyone put on their thinking-caps. When you make something sound too important, people are afraid to make a decision. So when I can, I try to make sure that my voice is light-hearted, almost nonchalant.

His advice is a warning of what can happen if we are too intense. But if we are over anxious to put ourselves or the other person at ease, too much time is often wasted and then the real business has to be rushed.

David Jacobs is chairman of the weekly BBC programmes *Any Questions* and *Any Answers*. There is a different panel each week so he is always meeting new people. He told me he makes 'social sounds' to help them relax: 'Did you get here all right?', 'Have any trouble parking?', 'Did you come up from London?' But he never lets this go on for more than a minute or two or it would detract from the purpose and quality of the encounter.

The way we set up a meeting can help. A producer telephoned an impresario:

Producer   Can you spare me fifteen minutes of your time?
The impresario agreed, suggested a day and asked what time would be convenient.
Producer   What time do you leave for home?
'6.45' came the answer.
Producer   If it's all right with you, I'll come at 6.30.

The other man would be more relaxed because the day's work was done. He would know the meeting wouldn't drag on and that the point would be reached quickly.

In someone else's office, we are at a disadvantage: it's another man's territory. But the other man can help. The producer recalled with warmth how the impresario got up from behind his desk and came forward to meet him.

It is a great opportunity to talk to someone face to face. You have an advantage you can never have with a letter. A letter goes out blind: you're not there to see how the other person reacts and the best you can do is to anticipate hang-ups and doubts. When someone is in front of you, there is a chance to spot a misunderstanding and put it right before it becomes a block. You can see when a point needs making again. If you are helping someone, you can give comfort and encouragement the moment you see anxiety and fear.

All that is lost if we think only of ourselves and what we are saying. When we are carried away by what we want, the other person usually gets left behind.

Even many famous people are nervous at face-to-face encounters, no matter how well they cover it up. Some people avoid them whenever possible and write letters instead, thereby missing valuable opportunities. It helps to think of an interview or a meeting with someone as the greatest chance in the world for real communication, because that's what it is. And we usually get through more successfully when we try to be ourselves—here's Margaret Thatcher again: 'I am what I am and I will stay that way. I just hope to improve in communication as I go along.'

When you talk to someone from behind a desk, that lump of teak or mahogany between you can be a real barrier, if you let it, and interfere with good face-to-face communication; just as a platform or a microphone can separate speakers from their audience.

In David Jacobs' home in London there is a message, finely engraved in italic script, from Ed Murrow the American broadcaster and war correspondent:

> The fact that your voice is amplified to the degree where it reaches from one end of the country to the other does not confer upon you greater wisdom and understanding than you possessed when your voice reached only from one end of the bar to the other.

David Jacobs, who spends a lot of his time before a microphone, has hung that message where he couldn't miss it—just behind the lavatory.

10 When to keep quiet

Words can work wonders but there are times when we should hold them back, when we get the result we want by saying less or even nothing at all. The best way to deal with some letters is not to reply to them.

In the hardest, toughest negotiations a knowledge of when to keep quiet can lead to success. If you doubt that, think back to the last time you came out of a meeting or an interview or hung up the telephone and were left with an uneasy feeling that you had said too much. Take heart if that has ever happened to you because it has happened to nearly everyone. It is reported that Joe Haines, former press secretary to Sir Harold Wilson, believes that during the October 1974 election his boss appeared on television too often. Anyone can make the mistake of saying too much.

We are so accustomed to noise, verbiage and instant comment on everything that we seriously undervalue silence. There are many practical situations in which things go better for us, or we help someone else much more, simply by keeping quiet. Here are six cases, as usual in this book, taken from real life:

The Service Manager
The service manager in a big garage was looking for a way to increase productivity by changing the system of work-flow. He called in his three best fitters to get ideas.

He explained the problem and then gave his own solution in some detail. When he asked for suggestions nothing much came forth and he was left with his own ideas.

Some time afterwards, he learned that the other men did not see much point in thinking too hard about the problem because he had already come up with a solution and they were reluctant to cut across that. He said it was a lesson to him in when to shut up.

If we are trying to get someone's ideas about anything, from a production control system to how to repair our washing-machine, we should be careful about rushing in with our own suggestions. Peter Brook tells us that no theatre director, whatever his capabilities, can understand a character in the same way as an actor who is actually playing the part:

> . . . one has to be very careful in the early stages not to trample on any fragile and instinctive buds that are sprouting.

Keeping quiet often creates an atmosphere that encourages other people's ideas to come to the surface.

The Social Worker

Kathy, a social worker, was troubled about a particular family in her area. It was difficult because she never had the chance to talk to any one of them on their own. One day she found Susan, the seventeen-year-old daughter, at home alone and Kathy seized the opportunity to ask some questions.

Susan was slow to reply and Kathy tried to help her by suggesting possible answers. The meeting did not lead any-where. Later on, Kathy saw that she had not given Susan time to think and to feel trust and confidence. She wished she had just waited quietly for answers to her questions.

Some clever and sensitive people ponder on problems and are often diffident about coming up with their own opinion, if another suggestion has been made. Others will try to say something different, even if they agree with a point of view, because they feel it is expected of them or they want to assert themselves.

When we see someone is thinking and trying to make the right connections, it is better to wait quietly instead of inter-fering with the process by talking.

It's the same the other way round. If you are the one who has to come up with an answer, be prepared to wait until you are ready. Our society puts a premium on quick thinking but it also values measured consideration. You can take your choice. Most people respond to someone saying, 'Would you mind if I think about this for a few minutes?' My solicitor once offered me a magazine to look at until he was ready with an answer to my question.

On radio and television it is always a rapid fire of questions and answers because there is no time to wait. But you have only to listen to the voices to know that these are contests of wit, not a search for wisdom and understanding. Sometimes the only honest answer to that over-anxious question 'Well, what do you think?' is 'I'm still thinking'.

The Secretary in the Ad Agency

Rosalind wanted a chance to be a copywriter. She tried her hand at writing advertisements and thought she had some good ideas. The next thing was to take them along to the creative director.

As he started reading what she had written, she explained why she had put certain things in and left others out, the purpose of the copy, whom it was aimed at and what other ideas she had discarded.

He put up with this for a while, then stopped reading and looked up:

It's better, Rosalind, either to write something down and let the other person read it. Or go along and tell them about it. But you have to choose. Otherwise who knows whether to listen or read? I've been trying to do both and not making a good job of either.

It is very common to ask someone to read a letter or a report, or to examine something, and to talk to them while they are doing it. We are often afraid not to fill the air with words even if those words get in the way.

Insecurity and uncertainty, the most common of all human feelings, make us say too much and write too much. The urge to justify ourselves is universal. Yet time and again by talking about our work and our ideas, unnecessary doubts come to the

113

surface. There are always doubts and it is often better not to stir them up.

Thor Heyerdahl says this about doubts and he should know, having drifted from South America to Polynesia on the Kon-Tiki raft and sailed across the Indian Ocean on a boat made out of reeds:

> There have been moments in my life when, if I had a mere second of doubt, I would never have done what I did. But if you do believe something, you can do it. The problem is to believe it.

There is no need to add to that problem by talking instead of keeping quiet.

The Personnel Director

Management and union were negotiating on a productivity deal. The personnel director discovered the shop steward had made a significant error in the calculations he had presented. He sent for him, showed him where he had slipped up and pointed out that such an error was irresponsible because it could cause serious disruption in industrial relations.

When the shop steward left the office, the personnel director had a nice feeling of self-satisfaction. But it didn't last very long. Within a few weeks there was an unofficial strike over some minor matter.

If something goes wrong there can be an almost irresistible urge to rub someone's nose in it. If we give way to it we often pay later on. It is a rule of human nature that when we make people feel inferior they have an instinctive drive to compensate.

'Be nice to people on your way up', the wise old statesman advised, 'you might meet them on your way down.' If that is too cynical and self-seeking for you, there is another way to see it. Generosity is one of the warmest of all human qualities. We have to tell people when things are wrong but we can choose to say it in as few words as possible.

The TV Writer

She had submitted an idea for a TV series to the head of a big television company in Los Angeles. As she explained it, she could see he was interested, especially when he began to talk back to her about the things he liked.

This encouraged her to go on building it up still further. Then she noticed that the curve of his enthusiasm was starting to turn downwards. Luckily she stopped in time. The TV series was made but she was convinced that if she had not kept quiet at that moment the idea might have been shelved.

In almost any discussion, when one person is trying to convince another, there is a peak. It is marked sometimes by the other person beginning to talk almost as if it is *their* idea. That's the moment to keep quiet, because after a peak the next direction must be downwards.

The Interviewer

Not one interviewer in particular but all those interviewers on television and radio who come between us and someone we want to listen to. This happens when the interviewer does most of the talking. An angry television critic wrote once, 'Television interviewers should be neither seen nor heard.'

Every time we catch ourselves interrupting someone it is a warning that we are probably not getting as much out of the conversation as we might be.

TV advertising time costs so much that some advertisers are afraid not to stuff every second with words. 'Many words lead to exhaustion' as Lao Tzu, the Chinese prophet, said. When we watch TV that's what it feels like sometimes. We yearn for a pause in the sound-track.

The absence of sound can have a powerful effect. An American public service commercial to counteract drug abuse did not use a single word. During thirty seconds of silence we watched an addict giving himself a fix. The effect was chilling and the warning against drug addiction more powerful than any words.

There are different ways of keeping quiet. Silence can be respectful or sympathetic or compassionate. We can be quiet because we want to give the other person a chance, or our silence can be morose or sullen and aggressive.

When silence is directed at offering help and understanding, it can only enrich a meeting. Macaulay, the nineteenth-century writer and politician, was said to have 'occasional flashes of silence that makes his conversation perfectly delightful'. Thomas Hardy said of someone, 'That man's silence is wonderful to listen to.' Of the theatre, Peter Brook says:

> We have largely forgotten silence. It even embarrasses us; we clap our hands mechanically because we do not know what else to do, and we are unaware that silence is also permitted, that silence is also good.

I know a composer who became a millionaire because most of his compositions were jingles for TV commercials. He lived in a world of tinkling pianos, tape-recorders and vocal groups. Once when he asked me a question there must have been a pause for all of five seconds while I thought about the answer. 'What's the matter?' he demanded anxiously. 'I can't stand these terrible silences!'

Dag Hammarskjold, as Secretary General of the United Nations, was surrounded by talk but believed it was a waste of human resources '. . . to talk merely because convention forbids silence'. He designed an oasis of silence for the UN headquarters in New York, a room to be quiet in for anyone who works at the UN or visits it.

Silence is an essential part of human relationships and the real quality of understanding between one person and another can be measured by the unspoken communication between them.

Here is a story of two people getting through to each other without words. It is told by John Georgiadis, leader of the London Symphony Orchestra, about the gala occasion to mark the ninetieth birthday of the conductor, Leopold Stokowski:

> The soloist that evening was a very beautiful Rumanian violinist. As we took our seats for dinner, there was a mild commotion at Number One Table.

'Why is the soloist sitting at Table Number Two?' a command-ing voice was heard to say.. 'I want her to sit opposite me at this table.'

The distance between the soloist and the conductor was reduced, but conversation wasn't easy with the noise of a hundred people eating and drinking.

Stokowski wrote something on his programme and passed it across the table to the soloist. She was confounded by the sight of one large solitary question mark.

She sent back her reply, from a girl of twenty to a magnificent man of ninety—an exclamation mark.

A psycho-analyst, who is especially warm and compassionate, says that she tries to allow herself what she calls the 'luxury and confidence of silence', when she is asked advice about a difficult personal situation. She finds that by leaving the question hanging in mid-air, the other person will sometimes see for themselves the only possible answer to their dilemma.

A marriage guidance counsellor has observed that 'most rows in families are caused by what someone says and that a row can often be prevented by listening rather than talking. But she adds that there is an all-important difference between listening and 'not answering'. Only if the feeling is right, does silence have a creative quality.

It is in the deepest of emotional experiences that words seem most out of place. A man heard that his closest friend had been killed in a car crash. He went at once to his friend's wife. When she opened the door, they went together into the kitchen and he sat with her, holding her hand, for half an hour. Then he left. During his visit, nothing was said but years later she still remembered the comfort and sympathy that came across.

A mother and daughter had not seen each other for three years and during that time there had been joy and sorrow in both their lives. When they met in the arrivals lounge at the airport, the mother put her hands on her daughter's shoulders and held them firmly for what seemed a long time. Only then did they embrace and talk to each other. The daughter said she would remember that greeting for the rest of her life.

The culture and pressures of our society encourage and in fact demand that we describe, discuss and pass instant verbal judgement on everything. The concept of the ineffable is unwelcome, because unless we can talk about something, we are inarticulate, ineffective and no use at all on a television programme. Yet the compulsive need to say something about everything can come between us and real feeling. The quality of response to art, music or to any experience can suffer if we feel an overriding obligation to say something about it right away.

Some letters are best answered by silence. An angry, vituperative letter has often done its job for the writer by letting the poison out of their system. There are other letters, described by the editor of the Writers' Guild journal as 'written in pure adrenalin'. Most of us have second thoughts and don't post them. If you receive one and are trying to think about how to reply, consider the alternative of saying nothing. We do no good, and might do harm to ourselves, by replying to letters of that kind. If anyone should feel uneasy about not writing back, remember that silence is not just passive. It has its own living quality and can have dignity, poise and courage.

We need words all the same to persuade, inform, comfort, encourage and to put our case to the next person. Words are the driving force of communication. Words get things done and that's what this book is all about. But though words can do so much for us, it is a rare and valuable talent to know when *not* to use them.

11 Good and bad English

Grammar has a place but it should not come between us and what we want to say. When it gets in the way of good sense, grammar should always give way and let us move more freely and easily among the words and sentences of the most successful language of the twentieth century. For we cannot make good use of words if we have hang-ups about them.

When we use words naturally, they communicate better. If we strain to make our English absolutely 'correct', it is no guarantee that we shall get through to people. A hundred years ago, Henry Alford wrote a book called *The Queen's English*; it was Queen Victoria of course. His style is old-fashioned but his heart was in the right place:

> Aim at satisfying the common sense of those who read and hear, and then, though any one who has no better employment may pick holes in every third sentence, you will have written better English than one who suffers the tyranny of small critics to cramp the expression of his thoughts.

For far too long English was in the frigid grip of Latin and Greek scholars who made the running. Even by 1870, the study of English, as English, didn't count for much. There were no professors of modern English at Oxford or Cambridge; at Eton the English teacher came below the teacher of French and at Marlborough—behind the dancing master. All grammar was based on Latin and Ancient Greek, perfect languages for grammarians because they are dead languages and rules can be fixed.

This is the source of many tired old commandments like these:

Never begin a sentence with a conjunction like 'and' or 'but'.
Never end a sentence with a preposition such as 'with', 'on', 'to' or 'for'.

119

Never ever split an infinitive even if you have to turn a double-somersault to avoid it.

The Authorised Version of the Bible, translated by forty-seven of the best scholars at the time, begins:

> In the beginning God created the heaven and the earth. And the earth was without form and void; and darkness was upon the face of the deep. And the spirit of God moved upon the face of the waters. And God said, 'Let there be light': and there was light. And God called the light day, and the darkness he called night. And the evening and the morning were the first day.

After that, need we worry any more about beginning a sentence, a paragraph or even a chapter (as Charles Dickens did) with that old Anglo-Saxon word 'And'? Yet only recently a copywriter in a top advertising agency had a battle with a client who insisted it was wrong.

The copywriter gave in because the next battle was more important. He had written:

> There are a lot of extras you don't have to pay for.

The client said you can't end a sentence with a preposition—change it to:

> There are a lot of extras for which you don't have to pay.

The copywriter asked the agency's research department for help. Ninety per cent of the people who were shown both sentences said the client's version sounded unnatural and they had to think about it. The client backed down.

There are two ways to look at English. One view is that there is (or should be) a fixed grammar with definite rules: the other view is that the rules of our language are, at the last judgement, based entirely on usage, how English is used by most people in writing and speaking.

Even good scholars get mixed up about this. H. W. Fowler, who wrote the classic *Modern English Usage*, is sometimes treated like the judge in a linguistic supreme court. Yet he refused 'to assume autocratic control of the language, and put to death all the words and phrases that do not enjoy our approval'.

That is open-minded. But the same man proclaimed 'Americanisms are foreign words and should be so treated'. Take that to the heart and we throw out: gatecrasher, debunk, teenager, bulldoze, babysitter, crank, bluff, boom, slump, stunt, paperback and thousands of other useful words. Recently a professor from London University and a professor from Princeton agreed that 'the two varieties of English have never been so different as people have imagined, and the dominant tendency, for several decades now, has clearly been that of convergence and even greater similarity'.

All the evidence shows that English will never let itself be bossed about by anyone. The Society for Pure English, started in 1913 to guide the use and development of the English language, is as dead as a doornail. The Advisory Committee on Spoken English, set up by the BBC with men like Bernard Shaw and the Poet Laureate as members, gave up in 1938. Lord Reith, then head of the BBC, spoke its epitaph: 'There are no experts—only users.'

If there are enough of us, the way we use English will drive a coach and horses through any set of rules that any professor of English lays down. All of us who use the language help to make it. As in many things in life, the people to listen to are the doers rather than the teachers.

For Alistair Cooke, 'syntax may go to hell' so long as he sounds like 'one man talking to another'.

Bernice Rubens, the first woman to win the Booker Prize (in 1969 for her novel *The Elected Member*), says:

> Grammar to a writer is a total irrelevance. If I start thinking about grammar, I get caught up in the *how* instead of the *what* . . . grammar is a stranglehold on passion.

She added this in a note to me:

> But before a writer discards grammar, he must know it intimately. He must at one time have loved it. He must *always* respect it. Only then is its irrelevance clear and logical.

Collett, Dickenson, Pearce is the London ad agency that is

famous because it wins so many creative awards. John Salmon, the creative director, answered my question about grammar:

> I only think about grammar if I am reading some copy and something brings me to a halt. It might be the grammar that sounds wrong or a peculiar word or just a clumsy sentence.

Carlos Slienger, an American/Mexican publisher and writer on political economy, shrugged when I asked him about grammar:

> Language is by definition functional. I never think about grammar; I am interested only in the flow of ideas. If someone says to me 'That's bad grammar', I reply 'Oh sure!'

And Winston Churchill wrote in the margin, when someone clumsily avoided ending a sentence with a preposition, 'This is the sort of English up with which I will not put!'

Even Noah Webster, who recorded every word he could find in his great *American Dictionary of the English Language*, admitted:

> Language is like the course of the Mississippi, the motion of which is at times scarcely perceptible yet even then it possesses a momentum quite irresistible. Words and expressions will be forced into use in spite of all the exertions of all the writers in the world.

Yet somehow it does not become a free-for-all. English has to have a structure or it would become sloppy. Many people feel a responsibility towards this. Capital Radio, the independent radio station for London, has a lot of influence on the way English is used. 'Certain things drive me bananas', John Whitney their managing director said to me, 'When, for example, announcers say *excetera* for etcetera or *garridge* for garage, I get someone to mention it to them. Why should we teach half London to pronounce words wrongly?'

All good writers and speakers play a part in keeping the structure of English in place. But it is a light framework supporting the language, not heavy chains that shackle it. About this, there can be no more authoritative voice than Sir James Murray's, the stern bearded Victorian, first editor of the *Oxford English Dictionary*:

. . . there is absolutely no defining line in any direction: the circle of English has a well-defined centre but no discernible circumference.

There is freedom in the way we can use English; there is also some order. The balance between the two is delicate and no one has the right to lay it down for all time and for everyone. History has shown that our language has its own instinctive genius and can take good care of itself. English picks out with almost chemical certainty what is suitable for it.

In dictionaries English words are usually divided into four categories.

Standard English: Words that are used even in the most formal situations.

Colloquial (usually abbreviated *colloq.*): Words used in everyday speech. Many are used in writing and in formal speech so it is hard to distinguish them from standard English.

The BBC, who give a lot of thought to language, use in official news bulletins 'pub', 'shambles', 'phone', 'boss' and many other words that dictionaries generally list as *colloq.*

Slang (usually abbreviated *sl.*): These words are less generally acceptable although they are understood by nearly everyone.

Some people never use them at all, even in their relaxed moments; and this gets them into trouble. Try finding a better word than 'hangover' (*sl.*) to describe how you feel the morning after.

The *Concise Oxford Dictionary* doesn't help. It tells you that 'hangover' is slang. You look up 'morning after' which it says is colloquial and means 'hangover'.

Vulgar (usually abbreviated *vulg.*): Words that make your maiden aunt and a lot of other people blush. The famous four-letter words come into this category.

According to the COD* these words are 'used only by those who have no wish to be thought polite or educated'. That's a slap in the face for the BBC, a number of leading novelists on

---

* COD—*The Concise Oxford Dictionary*, 1976 edition. References from here on to standard, colloquial and slang are the decisions of that dictionary.

both sides of the Atlantic, many critics and journalists and some good poets like W. H. Auden and Philip Larkin.

The lines dividing these categories keep moving. *Colloq.* today becomes standard tomorrow. This year's *sl.* moves up to *colloq.* next year. The COD shows 'upbeat' and 'downbeat' as good standard words although they are not even listed (apart from reference to a musical term) in the much larger 1959 *Shorter Oxford English Dictionary.* 'Up the spout' is standard but 'up the creek' is slang. 'To make a hash of something' is standard although if you 'settle someone's hash' you're colloquial.

As for all those *vulg.* words, there is not much you can find on the walls of public loos (*colloq.*) that you cannot also read in serious novels and poetry and hear in theatres in Shaftesbury Avenue and on Broadway.

We need dictionaries and can all be grateful to those who slog away at compiling them. They help us to find our way through the jungle of words. But a lot of things, even in the best dictionary, can be no more than the opinion of the editor.

Just as so many old-established traditions in society are on the blink (*sl.*), so is the use of English. Words are changing their meanings and their status quicker than ever before. 'After two months of uninterrupted intercourse', wrote Elizabeth Barrett Browning on her honeymoon in 1846, 'he loves me better every day . . . and my health improves too.' She would hardly write that now.

We cannot call slang bad English—G. K. Chesterton said it is 'the one stream of poetry that is constantly flowing'. Carl Sandburg, the American poet born in Illinois, wrote:

> Slang is language which takes off its coat, spits on its hands and goes to work.

If we want our words to do that, it is up to us to decide what words turn us on (*sl.*) and do the job we want. At a board meeting of a well known public company the chairman used the most familiar of all the four-letter words to cut through the veneer of politeness that was holding up progress.

English can be all things to all people in their drive to express what they think and feel. Shakespeare twisted and stretched words to make them do what he wanted. Three hundred years later the American writer, Damon Runyon, invented Runyonese out of slang used by Brooklyn crooks. Runyon is treated as a serious writer.

In the 1890s someone came out with the perfect word 'skyscrapers' to describe the tall buildings going up in New York. In the 1960s John Lennon played around with words to arrive at 'The Beatles', the most successful name for any group. Our language is freer now, more open and more available. If you make sausages and you want to call your product 'The Posh Sausage', go ahead. One manufacturer did and it looked good on posters.

If our words are not understood or are unsuitable at the time, in the place or the situation, they are bad English, because they do a bad job. When Edward Heath was Prime Minister his speech writers gave him a list of 'words to avoid, because meaningless to the majority of the audience'. In that context, they would have been bad English.

It is bad English to ask the waitress in a transport café for some of 'the cup that cheers but not inebriates' (William Cowper). Although it might be good English, if you don't mind sounding pompous, to make the same request to your host at tea-time in the senior common room of an Oxford college.

In the transport café you will get what you want by asking for 'A cuppa char, please', which, if it comes naturally to you, is perfectly good English in that situation, although you would get very low marks if that's what you ask for at a royal garden party.

'Smoking can kill' is good English. 'Every packet carries a Government health warning' is codswallop (*sl.*). Charles Saatchi, head of the London advertising agency that handles the anti-smoking campaign, pointed out that 1979 posters and advertisements for Benson and Hedges cigarettes used no other words except the obligatory Government health warning. The advertisers must have been confident nobody would bother with that—even when there was nothing else to read.

It was bad English when this notice appeared on some London buses:

> Passengers are requested not to communicate with the driver while the vehicle is in motion.

Now they have changed it to good English:

> Please do not speak to the driver while he is driving.

The doors in a Government building carry this notice:

> This door must not be left in an open position.

Some day they will put it into good English— 'Please shut the door'.

The purpose of language is to move ideas as freely as possible from one mind to another. That is the acid test of anything we write or say and it should be applied ninety-nine per cent of the time.

The other one per cent covers the use of language in creative writing or mysticism. Poetry does not have the obligation to be immediately clear. Sometimes we have to work to sense the imagery of a poet and the reward is an enrichment of our feelings and understanding, an aesthetic experience. The writings of mystics concern a spiritual perception of truth which we glimpse only in flashes of revelation.

When English is used in those ways it belongs to an inner world. But most of us live in the outer world. Here if we make others struggle to understand what we are writing or saying, it is bad English, rotten to the core.

Professor Alan C. Ross, the philologist, analysed the difference between upper-class and non upper-class English— 'U' and 'Non-U'. Among Professor Ross's 'Non-U' expressions are:

> Suit yourself
> Don't give up
> That's right (for 'Yes')
> It's as simple as that

126

When it comes to the crunch
Believe you me
It's just one of those things
I'll go along with that
Back to square one.

Before you drop any of those phrases, remember they are all used in Oxford and Cambridge common-rooms, both Houses of Parliament, the Courts of Law, the White House and from the pulpits of churches.

As for errors in grammar, there's hardly a writer anywhere who has not been picked on for making mistakes.

It is a great help to be aware of good English usage. When we know the rules we can depart from them with more confidence. But there is no need to be over-anxious about it. Our ear and our commonsense can help us to get through to people; and nothing else matters as much.

But here is a warning. Some people are very up-tight (*sl.*) about anything they consider the slightest linguistic mistake. They stick by what they were taught at school twenty, thirty or forty years ago. Luckily most people go along with a wide range of personal choice in the use of language. We can use our feelings and our own judgement to guide us. In a company report, English that seems too easy-going might not inspire confidence. In a letter to a customer, a friendly conversational style might be just the job (*sl.*).

We always get through to someone better using words we feel comfortable using and they feel comfortable reading or listening to. There is no need to try to be with it (*sl.*) if that's not your style. But a too careful use of language takes all the guts (*colloq.*) out of it.

If necessary, you can look something up in Eric Partridge's *Usage and Abusage* (available as a Penguin). It's a carefully compiled dictionary of grammatical and linguistic points, although you might find it conservative and rather old-fashioned.

The Complete Plain Words is a more friendly and open guide, even though it was written for the Civil Service and published by Her Majesty's Stationery Office. It accepts that there is a generous margin of tolerance about whether something is good English. Perhaps that's because Sir Ernest Gowers who wrote it and Sir Bruce Fraser who revised it spent their lives, not as scholars and linguistic experts, but using English every day to get through to people.

A dozen problems over the use of English came up regularly in my discussions with directors of companies, executives, engineers, secretaries, doctors, journalists and copywriters. As so many people have doubts about these points, here are some guide-lines on how to cope with them.

These are offered in the spirit of friendliness rather than dogmatism. They are not signposts telling you exactly where to go but a map of the territory to help you find the routes that suit you best. They are based on current usage by good writers including prize-winning novelists, poets, writers for *The Times*, the BBC and the *New Yorker*.

Contracted forms

Forms like I'm, it's, I'll, isn't and can't. We all use them in conversation but some people hesitate to use them in writing.

Written and spoken English are becoming closer to each other all the time and these contractions have been seen in formal letters from the Post Office, solicitors, MPs, the London Electricity Board and English and American universities.

Serious novelists like William Trevor and Saul Bellow (who won the Nobel Prize for Literature in 1977) use them not only in dialogue but in narrative.

If it seems laboured to write these forms out in full all the time, the way is wide open to use a contraction when you feel like it. But if you overdo it, it can sound sloppy.

Distinguish, of course, between 'its' and 'it's': 'It's a good thing its owners have returned.' ('It's' means 'it is'; 'its' is the possessive of 'it'.)

Corporate words

Words like the company, the board, the firm, the department, the government. Do we say 'The board has decided' or 'The board have decided'?

Either will do in most cases. But you can't have it both ways and write: 'The board *has* not yet given *their* decision.' Choose between 'has' and 'its decision'; or 'have' and 'their decision'.

When you're talking about the individual members of the board, firm, and so on it is more natural to treat the word as plural:

The board are now having lunch.
The committee are not getting anywhere.

When it's the body as a whole it's easier to treat it as singular:

The board has given a ruling.
A committee has been appointed.

Different from and different to

'Different to' is all right (*The Oxford English Dictionary* quotes it and you can't ask for more) but a lot of people think it is wrong.

Lord Ted Willis, the writer, was challenged in a radio programme by his neighbour—'Surely, Mr Willis, you mean different *from*.'

'If you're going to be pedantic about it,' came the answer, 'call me *Lord Willis*.'

'Different than' is all right too (*The Concise Oxford Dictionary*) and is frequently used in the US.

Got

Some people think the word is ugly. It is sometimes unnecessary. But that's not the same as saying it's wrong which a lot of people believe.

Shakespeare, Swift and Ruskin used it. Dr Johnson used it in a letter to Boswell. One scholar (Dr P. B. Ballard) said:

The only inference we can draw is that it is not a real error but a counterfeit invented by schoolmasters.

'Have you got some in stock?' is down to earth. 'Do you have some in stock?' is more elegant. You can take your choice. But don't be afraid to use 'got' when it suits you.

American usage is different.

Hyphens

The style-book of the Oxford University Press, New York, says, 'If you take hyphens seriously you will surely go mad.' Now you've been warned, let's continue.

The tendency is to drop the hyphen as soon as a combined word becomes familiar: air-strip — airstrip, space-suit — spacesuit, ice-cream—icecream. But sometimes it gets stuck: bus-stop, week-end, coffee-pot (although teapot).

You must do your own thing and if you write coffeepot, weekend and tea-pot, nobody should make a fuss about it.

There is no need to put a hyphen after 'co' in words like coordinate and coefficient, unless the word looks odd without one—co-director, for example.

Most words like readjust, reappraise, reassess, rework are used without hyphens although many people prefer to put one in.

If it looks right to your eye, that's as good a guide as any. But be careful about confusion of meaning: if you've lost your umbrella you want to recover it; if it's worn out it might be worth re-covering. Look out for this kind of thing. Otherwise relax.

-ise and -ize

People hesitate over words like realise, rationalise, organisation, utilise.

Usage and Abusage takes a hard line. If you followed it you would write 'advertize' which is not the way it's spelt in ad agencies in London or on Madison Avenue. *The Complete Plain Words* makes it easy:

> The simplest course is to use an *s* in all cases, for that will never be wrong, whereas *z* sometimes will be.

In the US it's usually the other way round—*z* is used most times, although there are a few exceptions.

Punctuation

Nearly everyone has a question about punctuation. Some people worry about it a lot and unnecessarily. Even experts say it is a matter of taste and common sense rather than rules.

If you think of the reader, you will avoid sentences like this one in *The Times*:

> When it rains women will wrap themselves as elegantly and with the modernity of chocolate boxes.

A comma before 'women' would have stopped us doing a double-take.

The style now is to use less commas and more full stops. Recently the experienced copy director of an ad agency was looking at a new copywriter's work. 'A comma?' he said, 'You're being rather grand, aren't you?'

Many people never use semicolons or colons. But a semicolon (which is halfway between a comma and a full stop) is sometimes useful to avoid too many short sentences.

If you want to find out more, there's a good chapter on punctuation in *The Complete Plain Words*. Otherwise try reading aloud what you have written and you'll usually see whether a comma is necessary to help someone get the message (*colloq.*) easily.

Shall and will

There is a definite rule taught by English teachers. Briefly, it prescribes that the simple future is: 'I' or 'We' 'shall'; 'He', 'she' or 'they' 'will'. Americans have for years used 'will' right across the board and English practice is now following that.

The Director of National Savings writes 'As requested I will send a warrant for £ . . .' No one should say this is wrong although some of us would prefer 'I shall send . . .'

In a few years' time 'I shall' may sound old-fashioned. There is a loss of subtlety of meaning when we drop the distinction between 'I will' and 'I shall', and so on, but that is the way the language is going. It is up to you to choose when to follow it.

Slang

Many people avoid good vivid expressions because they think they are slang, although some of them might turn out to be standard English.

131

There is no fixed rule. You can compare it to clothes. Some wear jeans and sloppy Joes at Covent Garden or at the Metropolitan Opera House, New York (the Met.). For others anything less than full evening dress would feel wrong.

Before you give up the idea of using a word or a phrase because you think it's slang, look it up. You might find it was used by Shakespeare and has been in the language for donkey's years (*colloq.*).

Split infinitive

This is the most well-known rule in English grammar and it goes on worrying people. Some regard it as the worst possible manners like eating peas off a knife. Bernard Shaw thought it was nonsense. The argument goes on and will probably always be with us. An infinitive is 'to' followed by the verb as in: to run or to write.

If you want to give special stress to a word, it can be useful to place it between 'to' and the verb: 'I want you to slowly walk across the room'. That gives 'slowly' more emphasis than 'I want you to walk slowly across the room'.

The enlightened view is that if you split an infinitive in order to express something clearly and naturally, no one should object. But someone will. That's the way it is.

Unisex pronoun

This is a real problem in English since the liberation of women. Take this sentence:

> If you are writing a letter to someone, you should make sure he understands it.

'He' means he or she; and that was all right at one time. But now women do not want to be included under 'he' or 'him'. The women helpers of OXFAM recently objected to the slogan 'OXFAM—Friends of Mankind' because they weren't keen on being lumped together under 'Mankind'.
Current usage accepts:

> If you are writing a letter to someone, you should make sure they understand it.

132

The objection is that 'someone' is singular and 'they' is plural. But 'they' is the most convenient unisex pronoun we have in English and it is frequently used, like chairperson and spokesperson, to overcome the difficulty.

There is nothing new in this. In the nineteenth century, Thackeray wrote 'Nobody prevents you, do they?' There is no other satisfactory way round it, unless you want to write 'he or she' all the time; and you and your readers would soon get tired of that.

Who and whom

Even the best writers get snarled up over this. *The Complete Plain Words* quotes Addison, the Bible, Shakespeare, Churchill and many others who have run foul of grammarians.

Does it matter? Some say it does very much. Others say that 'whom' is just a nonsense.

If you are confident that you can always distinguish properly between the subjective and the objective cases in English grammar, go on using 'whom' whenever it is appropriate. Otherwise it is safer to use 'who' most of the time, but expect to be picked up for it occasionally.

'Whom' already sounds pedantic and old-fashioned in speech. Some of us have a respect for it in writing. But in time 'whom' may become a linguistic drop-out (*colloq.*) in writing as well.

The notes on those problems attempt to be sensitive to the movement of the language. All changes are not for the better; some things are lost on the way. We can all play a part in trying to preserve the best, although it's not always easy to know what the best is because English has to work for a lot of different people. All over the world our language is being stretched in new directions and that is life-giving. W. H. Auden wrote:

> Time . . .
> Worships language and forgives
> Everyone by whom it lives.

The last words can be left to Isaac Bashevis Singer who was awarded the Nobel Prize for Literature in 1978:

> I think the only reason languages disappear is when they lose any creative power.

If that's the case, English is going to be around (*colloq.*) for a long time to come.

12 Putting it all together

A check-list for successful communication

This final chapter draws together all the threads so we can see the pattern of successful communication. A communication between one person and another can be a living thing or stone-cold dead. This applies in business, politics, personal relationships and in every encounter with another human being.

Here is simple proof of this by an international advertising agency. They make up a batch of a product in plain wrappers. Half the wrappers have one slogan on them and the other half another. Two packets, each with a different slogan, are given away to three hundred housewives.

A week later someone calls on every woman and asks which of the supposedly different products she liked better. Usually over eighty per cent have a preference. As the two products are identical, only the words on the packet could have created the difference.

If we remember that test every time we write an important letter, pick up the phone or talk to someone face to face, we shall never take for granted the words we use

Making words work can become a habit. Until then, a glance at the following check-list will help to keep you on the right track.

1 What do you want to happen next?

This is the most important question for any communication. If it is not asked right at the outset we leave our words to chance. The answer is not always self-seeking; there are times when we want someone to feel comforted, reassured or loved.

In a communication we work backwards from Newton's Law that every action has an equal and opposite reaction. We decide the reaction we want and work back to the words that will produce it.

135

Faced with a blank sheet of paper, a recording machine or an attendant secretary, it's easy to get stuck with the question 'What do I want to say?' Katharine Whitehorn, the journalist, thinks that offices and conference rooms 'are jammed with people, half of whom dictate an endless stream of letters and memos and draft documents on to the notepads of the other half, who are secretaries too stunned to protest'.

Everywhere the wastage in wordpower is overwhelming. It is like running an airline with no fixed destinations so you board an aircraft without knowing where it is going to land.

The way out of this is to define the result we want as clearly as possible before we start writing or speaking. From that moment on, our words work in an entirely different way.

Alternatives dissipate energy. The human mind needs a definite basis for making a decision and we help someone when our attitude is consistent and positive.

When you focus on the results you want, you pick the words that get through for you and leave out all the others.

2   Would you say that to someone you know?

Every story of successful communication has at the heart of it a real contact between one person and another. Ronald Kirkwood, one of the most well-known creative men on the London advertising scene, says, 'The best advertisements are those that recognise and take advantage of the opportunity to have a private conversation with someone.'

Before you put a word down, before you go into an interview, before you dial a number, think about the other person. If you are wrapped up in yourself, instead of communicating you are out there on your own.

John Whitney, head of Capital Radio, receives many letters. Some are written as if he were the head of the BBC. Although he tries to deal with all letters fairly, he says he cannot help being put off by a letter that shows no awareness of the job he is doing, running a lively independent radio station.

It is often a good idea to read your letter out loud to hear what it will sound like to the other person. David Abbott, who some copywriters say writes the best copy in London, tells us:

> I always read my copy out loud . . . I often find I'm speaking out loud as I write. Do this and you'll get copy that flows, not to mention a reputation as a moron.

3 Have you made a good start?

It is a basic law in advertising that no advertisement is better than its headline. Tests show that a change in headline can make ten times as many people read the same ad.

Every communication has to start by getting the other person's attention; and the more attention it gets the better it gets through. If we could see a graph of someone's attention, like a cardiograph, as they are listening to us or reading our letter or report, we would work very hard on our opening sentence.

Of course the first thing is to get through to the right person. A lot of advertising is wasted because it's seen by people who cannot buy the product. 'Half the money I spend on advertising is wasted', said John Wanamaker, 'but I can never find out which half.'

We should try hard to find out who will take the responsibility to make the decision we require. The bigger the decision, the easier it is to know. A sign on President Truman's desk read, 'The buck stops here.'

The least we can do is find out the other person's name. 'Dear Sir' or 'Dear Madam' never turned on anyone.

Once we know the right person, we've won half the battle when we get their attention.

4 Have you bored the pants off them?

How much we can write or say depends upon how important it is to the other person because it is human nature for people to be more interested in themselves than in anything else. John Salmon, creative director of Collett, Dickenson, Pearce, wrote some of the most successful advertisements for recruiting army

137

officers. He wasn't worried, he said, about using a lot of words because 'when you are inviting someone to consider changing their career, they are prepared to read a good deal about it'.

But Edward Heath was given this warning about speaking on television: 'People are not used to hearing speeches in their living room. The same voice talking continuously for more than a minute or two creates a strain.' That's a good reason to avoid making speeches in letters or reports.

For W. H. Auden the severest test of a poem was to write it out in longhand. That can be a ruthless check at times on something we've dictated or typed.

A professor of English at Cornell advised:

> A sentence should contain no unnecessary words, a paragraph no unnecessary sentences, for the same reason that a drawing should have no unnecessary lines or a machine no unnecessary parts.

If we keep to that we are less likely to bore the pants off people.

5 Do your words have added value?

Our words always have added value when they appeal to someone's motives and interests. It does not have to be hard sell: it can be done with humanity and warmth and then people respond all the more.

Nearly every outstanding advertisement works because it focuses on one simple idea:

> A group of identical glasses with vodka and chunks of ice in them. One glass is in front. The words: If Vodka has no taste, how come I can tell which one is WOLFSCHMIDT?

> A picture of a wrinkled, smiling Indian—Western style. He is happily eating a sandwich. The words: 'You don't have to be Jewish to love Levy's real Jewish Rye.'

> A simple pencil outline of the VW 'Beetle'. Below it this question: 'How much longer can we hand you this line?'

When we are anxious about something, it is natural to focus on what we want. But if a letter or a conversation or a speech is full of 'I want' and 'I need', the words drop in value—to someone else.

I once saw a copy director turn down a piece of copy. 'Tell them what they want to know', he said to the writer, 'not what you want to say.'

6 Does the ending do something?

Your last sentence is your last chance to get through. The best endings are action endings. Some ads show a hand cutting out the coupon. That tells the reader exactly what to do next.

If you are talking or writing to your husband, father, daughter or a friend, your last words can be just as important. They can leave the other person feeling warm and wanted.

The worst endings are non-endings, when a letter or conversation peters out. Try covering up your last sentence. If you don't miss it, you should rewrite it. Our last words can make all the difference.

7 Remember psycho-linguistics

Words are loaded with feelings and emotions and can put people off without them knowing why. When you say the same thing in warmer words, they feel much better about it.

Where possible turn negative statements into something positive. 'We cannot meet your delivery date' is one thing. 'We can deliver for certain by . . . and we hope this will be all right for you' is something else.

We do not always need to spell out in detail all the negative aspects of a situation. People have enough doubts and fears.

When there is a dark side, it is better to explain it directly and clearly, rather than camouflage it; and then turn to reasons for hope and encouragement. Winston Churchill frequently did this in the desperate days of the last war.

Remember what happens when confidence in a company is affected: immediately their shares take a tumble. For once, politicians are right when they always talk of winning even when the odds are against them. Anything can change—'a week in politics is a long time'.

Words are full of positive and negative energy. So be careful of cold words. People cannot help being affected by them. Try to replace them by words that are warm and life-giving.

8   Have you said too much?

Talking or writing too much conveys uncertainty and insecurity to someone else. When we learn to pause, to be quiet, to write less, our words have time and space to work harder for us.

One of the tests of sentences in advertising copy is—'Do they have people nodding with them?' We should leave time for the other person to agree; then they might do half the work for us.

If a letter looks too long, it is useful to cover up each paragraph in turn to see if we're better off without it.

In every human activity, timing is paramount. Keeping quiet at the right moment can do everything we want.

9   Have you worked at it?

A successful ad man discovered that his son was dyslexic and needed special help at school. The one school that could give him that help was full. Although the boy's father is an experienced writer, he spent three weeks working over his letter to the headmistress. The reply came by return: 'After a letter like yours, how can I not see you?'

A good rule in advertising, when it's an important ad, is: Hold it for two weeks. In the States they say that rule can save millions of dollars. It gives someone a chance to think again and do more work on it.

The head of a successful company said to me, 'There are times when even the most brilliant executive must realise that the really clever course is not to be clever at all.' It takes time and work to be simple.

Most good writers are used to rewriting sentences many times to make sure they are really getting through. Keats's famous line 'A thing of beauty is a joy for ever' first appeared as 'A thing of beauty is a constant joy'. Not the same thing at all.

It's worth going over an important letter again and again. All the effort is worth while when it delivers the results you want.

10 Aim to be serious, not solemn

Russell Baker wrote an inspiring piece for *The New York Times Magazine*. He explained the difference between being serious and being solemn.

As I understand it, being serious is getting through to the heart of the matter. Being solemn is being heavy, laboured and self-important.

These are some of Russell Baker's examples. In politics, Adlai Stevenson was serious: General Eisenhower—solemn. In literature, Shakespeare above all is serious. In journalism, *Playboy* is solemn: the *New Yorker*—serious. Among cities, Washington is solemn: New York—serious.

To help you get the idea here are some more suggestions. Working out a system to break the casino at Nice or Cannes is serious: hijacking an aircraft with innocent passengers on board is solemn. A cheese soufflé (when it holds up) is serious: rice pudding must be solemn. Making love can be either serious or solemn: it all depends.

This report from an airline is very solemn:

In early 1976 we started out with clear research evidence that told us that improvements in the quality of the product delivered to our passengers were not mirrored in the perceptions of those passengers.

It could have been serious:

In early 1976 we found that passengers didn't know we were doing a much better job.

This headline from a recent OXFAM appeal is beautifully serious:

Doing nothing, that's death.
Helping people, that's life.

141

When we are serious we connect with the mainstream of human experience and feeling. When we are solemn we are out of touch and our words drag.

In the 140-odd pages of this book I must at times have slipped into being solemn. As Russell Baker says, it is hard to be Shakespeare. It's not all that easy to make a good cheese soufflé every time. It's hard to be serious. But it's always worth trying.

Thanks

The people who have helped

The experience, ideas and examples from the work of many people have gone into this book. It is only fair to mention the following:

David Abbott
Russell Baker—for the theme of his article 'Why Being Serious Is Hard' (*The New York Times Magazine*)
BBC, London—for letting me listen to tapes
The late Irving Berlin
Anthony Blond, publisher
Dr Edward de Bono—for some valuable concepts in his book *Wordpower*
British Airways: Richard C. Douglas, advertising manager, USA
Peter Brook, theatre director—for his experience of non-verbal communication and the value of silence
Roy Brooks Estate Agents: A. R. Halstead—for permission to quote some of the original Roy Brooks advertisements
Dr R. W. Burchfield, chief editor of the Oxford English Dictionaries—for a quotation from a letter from H. W. Fowler
Capital Radio, London: John Whitney, managing director—for giving time and help
Henri Cartier-Bresson—for his observation on photography
Nick Cole—for information about the spread of English throughout the world, from his article in *The Times*
The late Fairfax Cone
Alistair Cooke—for many lessons to us all in getting through to people
Dr Ernest Dichter, founder of the Institute for Motivational Research, New York
Doyle Dane Bernbach, New York
Eastern Airlines, Miami: Frank Borman, president
Foote, Cone & Belding, London: Brian F. MacCabe, president; Len Sugarman, creative director; Dolly Beshell and Peter Hobden, copywriters
Sir Bruce Fraser—for some useful guide-lines in his revised edition of *Plain Words* (HMSO)
John Georgiadis, leader of the London Symphony Orchestra—for permission to repeat his story about Leopold Stokowski
Professor A. H. Halsey, director of the Department of Social and Administrative Studies, University of Oxford
Lesley Howard—for help with research
Douglas Hurd—for information about politicians' speeches, from *An End to Promises* (Collins)

143

The Institute of Practitioners in Advertising
David Jacobs—for taking time to talk and listen to me
Ronald Kirkwood, The Kirkwood Company, London
Mary Wells Lawrence, chairwoman, Wells, Rich, Green, New York
The late Groucho Marx
Kay McManus, TV and radio writer
Dr David Mendel, consultant at St Thomas's Hospital, London—for some good advice on 'reading faces', from his article in *The Observer*
Jane Ellen Murray, associate creative director, J. Walter Thompson Company, Chicago—for the title of her article 'Would Your Daughter Want to Marry This Ad?'
Iain Murray—for facts about pin-up calendars
Hubert Nicholson, A. S. J. Tessimond's literary executor—for permission to quote Tessimond's poems *She* and *Daydream*, included in *Not love perhaps* . . . (Autolycus Press)
David Ogilvy—for comments on getting through and some good examples of doing it
OXFAM: Guy Stringer, deputy director
The late Eric Partridge—for quotations on slang; and reminders of catch phrases in *A Dictionary of Catch Phrases* (Routledge)
Lord Rothschild—for ideas in his lecture *Risk*
Bernice Rubens, novelist
Saatchi and Saatchi: Charles Saatchi, chairman; Len Barkey, director; Cecily Croke, James Lowther, Jeff Stark, copywriters
Norman W. Schur—for the schoolboy's description of cricket and valuable comments on Americanisms, from *British Self-Taught* (Johnston and Bacon, a division of Cassells)
Isaac Bashevis Singer, winner of the Nobel Prize for Literature 1978
Carlos Slienger, writer and publisher
Fritz Spiegl—for spotting the quotation from Elizabeth Barrett Browning's letter
The Right Reverend Mervyn Stockwood, Bishop of Southwark—for time and advice
Margaret Thatcher MP—for advice about nervousness and about not quoting too many facts and figures, from her conversation with Kenneth Harris printed in *The Observer*
The Times—for some quotations
Katharine Whitehorn—for comments about the problems of communication, from her article 'Mighty Quill' in *The Observer*
Woolwich Equitable Building Society: Donald Kirkham, general manager
The Writers' Guild of Great Britain
Young and Rubicam, Los Angeles and New York

Many others in the UK and USA (and some in Australia) have contributed real-life demonstrations of how to use words to get through. For these I am very grateful because we learn more from actual experience than from anything else.

GH

Index

146